GOD
CALLED
A GIRL

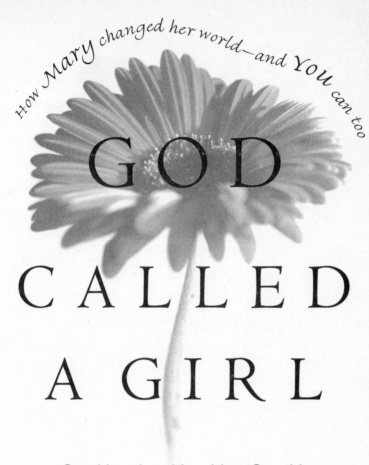

How Mary changed her world—and You can too

GOD

CALLED

A GIRL

SHANNON KUBIAK

BETHANYHOUSE
MINNEAPOLIS, MINNESOTA

Library of Congress Cataloging-in-Publication Data

Kubiak, Shannon.
    God called a girl : how Mary changed her world—and you can too / by Shannon Kubiak.
      p. cm.
    ISBN 0-7642-0029-1 (pbk.)
    1. Teenage girls—Religious life—Juvenile literature. 2. Mary, Blessed Virgin, Saint—Juvenile literature. 3. Christian life—Juvenile literature. 4. Conduct of life—Juvenile literature. 5. Spirituality—Juvenile literature. I. Title.
    BV4551.3.K83   2005
    248.8'33—dc22   2004020639

To my friends and family at CCM:

Thanks for always giving me a place to come home to,
and for reminding me, many times, that God called a girl.

And for my Lord and Savior:

There is not a day that goes by
I am not eternally grateful for
Your unfathomable love for me.
Thank You for calling me, equipping me,
and always having bigger plans for me
than I could ever have for myself.
May my life always be an offering back to You.
You are my first love.

In addition to being an author, SHANNON KUBIAK speaks at youth events around the nation and is on staff at her home church, where she teaches and coordinates the *Being a Girl* Bible study program. In her early twenties, she has a passion for helping other girls find their identity in Christ and pursue the purpose He has specifically outlined for them.

Shannon has a B.A. in Journalism and a minor in Biblical Studies from Biola University. She was the recipient of the North County Times Excellence in Writing Award in 2000 and the San Diego Christian Writers Guild Nancy Bayless Award for Excellence in Writing in 2003. She has also been featured on the PBS program *Religion and Ethics NewsWeekly* and in *Time* magazine. When she is not writing or speaking, Shannon can usually be found at one of San Diego's beautiful beaches or watching a baseball game.

Shannon enjoys hearing from her readers and would love for you to visit her at her Web site, *www.shannon kubiak.com*, or to e-mail her at *shannon@shannonkubiak.com*.

Contents

Introduction
IT ONLY TOOK ONE GIRL

Some people who pick up this book will probably think it is about Mary. Although it contains many insights into Mary's life, it is not really about Mary at all. This is a book about God and what He can do with one teenager fully committed to Him. Mary's life is merely used as a backdrop on which God's grace is brilliantly illuminated, despite waning human emotions and fears. This book highlights what happens when we let obedience rule our decisions and let God rule our lives.

God is looking for world changers. He found one in Mary; perhaps He will find one in you too. Every week I meet and receive e-mails from dozens of girls who are out there changing the world for Jesus Christ. Some of them don't even realize the impact they are having until it is pointed out to them.

Softly, and many times quietly, and almost always when people are not looking, these girls step forward and emerge from the shadows living lives that boldly point to Jesus. Their presence isn't even always noticed at first. They live lives that start as whispers and slowly grow into a loud roar. In this respect, they remind me of Mary.

Every girl I meet is different—yet we all have similarities that unite us. We have characteristics that define us. And each and every one of us has the potential to change our world if we let God work through us the way He worked through Mary.

When presented with choices, Mary made the right ones. Hers is a story many of us know all too well. But often we overlook the details hidden in the pages of her life because we are busy seeing what we have always been taught to see. We overlook the fact that before Mary was a mother—perhaps the most well-known mother of all time—she was just a girl.

Mary was one teenager who revolutionized society. Had she lived in modern times, scholars say she wouldn't have even been old enough to have a driver's license. But God looked down from heaven and placed His favor on Mary. Before she probably even realized what had happened, her life was forever altered and she brought us the King of the world.

What an awesome story. Too bad for Hollywood, God beat them to the script. Lucky for Mary, God had all casting rights; otherwise she might have lost out to a glamour girl like Hilary Duff or one of the Olsen twins. Mary wasn't a beauty queen like Esther or a widow like Ruth. Some would probably even say Mary was just a small-town kid. There was nothing significant about her until the moment the angel of the Lord stepped on the scene.

Uninvited and unannounced, this angel came to inform Mary of the great call God had on her life. And

although I am no angel and I cannot give you any spe-
cifics, I'm here to tell you the same thing. God has plans
for your life—big plans. You are called to be a world-
changer, a girl who will make a difference for the kingdom of God.

Most of us, though, live like God is not calling and
the world does not need changing. We believe the lie that
it's too early to be used by God to make an impact.
Because of this the world remains unchanged, and our
lives become an endless cycle of going to school, doing
homework, going to sports practice, going to youth
group, eating junk food, and not getting enough sleep.
Somewhere in the midst of living we lose sight of what
we are really living for. Every now and then we all need a
reminder that there is more to life than the world we live
in; this book is such a reminder.

On an afternoon not that long ago, when I was going
about the normal hustle and bustle of life, God took me
to a story I knew well and He taught me to see it with
different eyes. For the first time ever I didn't see Mary as
someone who had it all figured out, or someone who was
super spiritual.

The impact of her story didn't reside in Mary herself, but in the God who called her. It is the same with
us. Because she was so much like us, there is a lot she
can teach us. Yes, Mary had an incredible amount of
faith—but it doesn't mean she never doubted or got
confused.

Yes, Mary was blessed among women, as the Bible tells
us in Luke—but that doesn't mean she never encountered

disappointment or loneliness. Yes, Mary was loved and loved greatly—but that doesn't mean there weren't moments when she felt unloved. Mary had many moments like you and me where the path grew dim, life was hard, and she felt all alone. Yet God loved her and used her in mighty ways.

When Mary was born there was no earthquake, no lightning bolt, no angels blaring trumpets announcing that the world would one day be changed by this simple girl. She was from Nazareth. If there was a nowhere, Nazareth was the middle of it.

Nothing good ever came from Nazareth (John 1:45–46), at least not until God had His way in the life of one teenager who lived there. God delights in using uncommon heroes. In the end, it's never about the one who is called. It is about the One doing the calling. No matter what anyone tells you, it's not about you. It is about God—and He wants to use you to help get that message out.

Be part of something that will live longer than you ever will. Mary's impact was so great that the whole world still knows of her on a first-name basis over two thousand years later. Someone even played her in a box-office blockbuster (*The Passion of the Christ*) in 2004.

Although God called many great men of faith to incredible tasks in the past, there came a time when a man would not do. So ... God called a girl. And that girl changed the world. The same God is calling again, and this time He's calling *you*. Are you willing to step forward and answer that call?

1

FAVORED AND BLESSED

*"The angel said to her, 'Rejoice, highly
favored one, the Lord is with you;
blessed are you among women!'"*
—Luke 1:28 (NKJV)

I used to squeal with delight as my dad lowered the well-worn cardboard box from the rafters on Thanksgiving weekend each year, for inside the battered box was a precious treasure. The old nativity set had been in my family for decades, and the hand-painted figurines captivated me as a little girl. Something about the expressions on the faces of the statues drew me into the story and took me away to Bethlehem. Even now, the nativity set is my favorite thing on display at Christmastime, and I look forward to the day when the family heirloom will grace my own living room.

Mary was always one of my favorite figures to set out. Delicately I would place her in the straw next to the manger. She was radiant; she looked so beautiful with her long brown hair cascading down her shoulders, covered by a veil. She was absolutely elegant—well, except for the fact I was setting her in a barn beside some cows and donkeys. But the look on the figurine's face was one of awe and reverence as she looked down at the manger where the baby Jesus lay, her soft pink lips curled into a smile. The detail in her painted face brought her to life in my mind; her expression was so tender.

I always imagined the real Mary's face looked somewhat the same way. I have often wondered what ran through her mind that night, as she was one of the first to see the King of Glory. I tried to transplant myself back in time as a means of connecting myself with the one girl who was more connected to God than any of us can really understand.

It only took a moment for God to change the world. Everyone else was busy going about his or her daily routine, unaware that Mary's story had just been forever interrupted, and life—as the whole world knew it—was about to change. I imagine the scene this way (bear with me, I have a vivid imagination): Mary's dad was at work, and her mom may have been out at the market. Her siblings were tending to their own tasks, and her fiancé, Joseph, was out earning a living.

God watched from heaven that afternoon, as the stage He had been designing ever since the world began was finally set to His liking. He probably gave a slight nod as He turned to the angel Gabriel.

"Now," He said softly. "But wait," He added as Gabriel turned back to face Him. "Don't scare her; she will do just as you ask. So be gentle."

Gabriel nodded as he looked glory in the face one last

time before he set out to eternally alter the lives of mankind. Mary had no idea a miracle was on the way—and she most certainly had no idea it was on its way to her womb.

The Gospels tell us Mary was one who was favored and blessed. My first response was to grab a synonym finder to see just what that meant. To be favored means: to be preferred, chosen, privileged, the favorite, affluent, elite, and noble. To be blessed means: to be exalted, happy, glad, pleased, and contented.

Although those definitions seemed to fit perfectly with what Luke was saying, a few moments of rummaging through Mary's past is enough to show that most people did not see her that way. Mary was just a small-town girl. Not only that, she was a poor girl from a despised small town.[1]

Mary was a nobody, yet she found favor and blessing with God. How many times do we look in the mirror and find a nobody staring back at us? We often limit what God can do with our lives because we think our upbringing, our appearance, or our life is not a sufficient tool for the hands of God to use for His glory.

If Mary really was a nobody, all it took for God to make her "somebody" was one miracle on a lonely day when she was just going about her daily business. God's formula for success isn't found in some stuffy rule book. His chosen are not normally found in palaces (although sometimes He chooses to take them there, like He did Esther and David), and His favored are often those who have nothing to offer but one small life—the type of life nobody else notices until God steps onto the scene.

Yes, God called a girl once before and He will most certainly do it again. Mary lived a life of passion, purpose, and divine intervention. She lived a life no other girl in all of time will ever get to live. Birthing the Savior of the world was a one-time task, and it fell to a humble teenager in the middle of nowhere.

God could have beamed Jesus down to earth. He could have made Him a full-blown man instead of a baby. God could have done anything in order to redeem the world. Funny, isn't it? He chose the *least likely plan of all* in order to save mankind. God used someone a lot like you in order to reach you. He planted himself in the womb of a virgin in an attempt to get the world's attention. It was the unfolding of a miracle, and most people didn't even stop to watch. Even today some who hear of it simply yawn and give a polite smile.

Years later God is still trying to get the world's attention. And so it is *at you* He looks with favor and blessing. He sees what you do not see—that *you* are in the line of Mary. So as the world is passing you by, without even a glance, God is setting the stage.

"This girl is something," He says to the angels in His company. "She is a real gem."

Jesus smiles and pauses. "She reminds me of my mother."

Acts 17:26 says God appointed the very time and place each of us should live. As He mapped out the timeline for all of mankind, He penciled you in, here and now, for a reason. You have a divine purpose. God's signature is on your life, and beneath it heaven can read the words *favored* and *blessed.*

Before you rush to the mirror to see if I am telling the truth, let me warn you—most of the time human eyes see things differently than God does. Heavenly handwriting is not usually read on earthly ground, but it is God's identifying mark on those whom He has chosen. He sees it, He knows it is there, and He knows for what purpose it was written on your life. And as God was with Mary, so He will be with you.

We all have purposes—things that connect our hearts to God and bring His message of salvation just a little bit closer to those who surround us on earth. And we are all gifted differently for a reason. There are people you can reach with your life and your gifts that I could never reach, even if I tried every day for the rest of my life.

We may not know exactly what our purpose is at the moment, but we do know the *purpose* of our purpose: we are to glorify God with our lives and to use our gifts and passions as a means of worshiping Him and pointing others toward Him.

Some of us may reach the masses with our lives; others may only greatly influence a handful of people. But it's not the numbers that matter—it's the fact that we are impacting people for the kingdom of God. Luke 15:10 tells us that the angels rejoice every time one sinner repents. Never underestimate the value of impacting just one person. Their whole eternity could be altered as a result of your impact—that's a huge thing!

Other times, God wants us to reach more than one.

Recently, I found myself staring an incredible opportunity in the eye. *You couldn't possibly use me for that, Lord,* I thought. *That's way out of my league.*

NOTHING IS OUT OF YOUR REACH UNLESS GOD SAYS IT IS.

God answered me by saying, *Why wouldn't I use you for that? I'm God, I've called you and equipped you and I own the whole league—so nothing is out of your reach unless I say it is.* Think about that—nothing shall be impossible to us if God is in it. Wow!

GOD SUPPLIES THE GIFT AND MAKES THE DIFFERENCE

Aside from the recounting of the actual Christmas story, one of my favorite looks at the heart of God at Christmastime is found in a little book called *The Best Christmas Pageant Ever.*[2] If you have never read it, I suggest you go to a bookstore and hunt it out this coming Christmas. In the meantime, I'll give you a brief synopsis so you have something to look forward to.

The story chronicles the planning and production of an annual church Christmas play—but this particular year, instead of choosing the well-churched children to play the lead roles in the pageant, the director chooses to allow the unruly, obnoxious, and not well-churched Herdman kids to participate. Do you know anyone like that?

To make a long story short, the Herdmans had never heard much about the true meaning of Christmas, and they came from a background that left them more than a little rough around the edges. The planning of the pageant becomes what most people would consider a disaster, as everything seems to go wrong. Even the pageant itself brings with it some unconventional additions to the narrative of the birth of Christ—like one of the wise men bringing a ham to the baby Jesus in lieu of frankincense.

But near the end of the play we see unruly Imogene Herdman—the Mary in this pageant—with her big hoop earrings, her matted and tangled hair that hadn't been washed in weeks, and a bulging black eye, sitting in the spotlight holding the baby Jesus, sobbing like she never had before.

Yes, all of the regular churchgoers scoffed at her and thought her unworthy of portraying the mother of Jesus, but God had a plan for this girl all along. He brought her Christmas like He never had before. Just like He visited Mary, God visited unlovable Imogene Herdman and said, "This is My Son—He is My gift *to you*."

I know that story is fiction, but it brings up a good point. We look at Mary and we think of her as a saint. *I am nothing like Mary,* we think as we drag ourselves through life completely missing the point. Hello! Mary was chosen for no reason other than she was faithful to God. In a moment God turned the poor girl from out in the sticks into a world changer. So whether you feel like an Imogene Herdman or the real Mary of Nazareth, rest assured that God has called you and chosen you—no matter who or what you feel like inside.

God has a calling on your life so big you cannot even fathom it. That's why He gives it to you in pieces. Life comes together like a puzzle, and we are always left waiting for God to put down the next piece in His perfect timing. The key is learning to *trust* God in the process.

When Gabriel first appeared to Mary, he did not say, "Mary, you will give birth to the Son of God, who at twelve years of age will get lost on your family trip to the temple because He is so wise He will even leave the scholars amazed. Your husband, Joseph, will train Him to be a carpenter, and then at age thirty He will begin a ministry of healing the sick, raising the dead, and calming the raging sea. At thirty-three He will be brutally crucified but will save the souls of all of mankind by rising from the dead on the third day. Are you up for this task?"

No. Instead he came to Mary quietly and said, "The Holy Spirit will come upon you, and the power of the Highest will overshadow you; therefore, also, that Holy One who is to be born will be called the Son of God" (Luke 1:35 NKJV).

That's it. He came and told her she was chosen, and He told her what she was chosen to do. That is also how God works with us. God visits us when we are busily going about our daily routine, and He rests His hand on our shoulder.

"It's time," He says quietly. At this point, we are not always sure of what it is time for.

All of my life I wanted to be an author. As a child I always told elaborate stories. I never felt as if I was good with anything but words—so I desired to use words as a way of reaching people. Wanting to write a book was a far-off dream, something that would probably occur in the later years of my life, if at all. But on one June afternoon, when I was only twenty years old, God visited me while I was reeling from the fact that my summer job had fallen through.

I cried out to God many times in my confusion and desperation. *What am I going to do now, Lord?* I was lost. There was no good that I could see in my situation. When I quieted my racing heart, God answered my cry with an inner nudging: *You're going to write a book.*

I laughed, but when God didn't, I sat down at my computer, and my first book, *The Divine Dance*, was born. The book didn't come because of anything I did on my own, and it most certainly did not come because I had any experience (I was just a college student looking for something to do with my summer).

It came to me as a gift, packaged as a call on my life, the magnitude of which I only began to understand when the book was actually on store shelves a year later. God likes to show up in ordinary things and make them extraordinary. The ordinary part is us; God is everything extra. We simply need to make ourselves available to Him. What He does with our availability is up to Him.

And we should never measure our worth against what He is doing in the lives of others our age. He has different plans for each of us. So if you are a little ahead of others when it comes to finding your call in life, be thankful, but not boastful. If you feel as if you are a little behind, keep looking to God with an expectant heart; He will reveal His plan for you in His perfect timing. Perhaps you are not ready to see—or receive—it yet.

Sometimes people don't even realize what God is

doing in their lives at the moment. Some of us can only trace God's hand years later, when we're looking back. But rest assured, even if you cannot see God at work in your life today, He is there.

TWO PIVOTAL PIECES OF TRUTH

In the semester before I graduated from college, a well-known professor who taught for nearly three decades sat down with me as I interviewed him for the school paper. He was retiring at the close of the year, and the weariness in his eyes and the stoop in his step showed he was more than ready.

As he poured himself a cup of coffee before we began, I surveyed his well-used office. The white walls had yellowed, and piles of papers and stacks of books had collected layer upon layer of dust from having been untouched for so long. An older, now unusable word processor sat on the floor in the corner, telling the story of a career changed by all forms of technology. The wise old professor turned his cell phone off and set it on the table as he sat down and joined me.

"Where do you want to begin?" His voice was tired, but his eyes were smiling. In the next half hour or so he recounted to me nearly thirty years of wisdom he had gained at that institution.

Today, only two pieces of that wisdom remain with me. But they are two of the most valuable nuggets I ever received. First, he said, "You must never forget God wants to *use* you in the process of *blessing* you." I scribbled furiously as he spoke, and only later did I ponder just what that meant to me.

Secondly, when asked to describe the past thirty years of his life in three words, he said, "God is faithful."

I stopped cold. People normally answered with words like "fun," "challenging," and "rewarding" when describing their walk with God. Yet here this man sat, and without even hesitating he said, "God is faithful." The statement struck me in a way I will never forget because this professor had faced some difficult and painful things over the years, and those wounds were not easily hidden from the prying student body.

Age gave that professor wisdom that is sometimes missed by youth. God wants to use us in the process of blessing us. Just look at how He used Mary. The child she delivered grew up to be the One who delivered her from her sins. For nine months Mary housed the Savior of the world in her womb, and from the day He ascended to heaven, Jesus worked to prepare an eternal home for Mary.

God is faithful—He is always faithful, even when it doesn't seem like it. Yesterday I responded to an e-mail from an aunt who was seeking encouragement to pass on to her niece who is fighting to stay pure and strong in a wild and crazy world. The young girl is staying faithful, but she is also growing weary. My encouragement to her was this: *Be firm.*

> GOD WANTS TO *USE* YOU IN THE PROCESS OF *BLESSING* YOU.

Do not waver even for a moment on the commitment you have made to God—He will always be faithful to you; be faithful to Him in return.

My message is the same to you today. God has called you, He has gifted you, and He loves you with an everlasting love. Be faithful to the One who has always been—and will always be—faithful to you. You are chosen and blessed, just like Mary was. You don't have to understand why; just accept it and rise to the task at hand. God will delight in helping you along the way.

YOUR OWN UNIQUE ADVENTURE WITH GOD

Life is one big adventure with God. And He knows the path He has set you on like the back of His hand. He knows the bumps and the bends—and He is not worried about them. God knows your gifts and passions and their potential to bring Him glory. He knows the lyrics and the notes to the songs He wants you to perform. He knows the strokes He wants your pencil or paintbrush to make. He knows the words He wants you to type out on the page. He knows the child He wants you to influence as you baby-sit or tutor him or her each week. And He knows the prayer He wants you to say aloud as you and your team prepare to take the field before a crucial game.

God's daughters have many different passions, many different talents, and many different names. We are similar probably in only one way: we are all favored and blessed. Each of us is called by God to bring glory to God. *Okay,* you may be thinking, *so I am favored and blessed. How am I supposed to find out what God wants me to do with my life now? At least Mary had an angel who laid it all out for her.*

If you are asking a question like that, you are in the right place. Later on in the book we will talk about Mary's willing response to God's plan for her life, but for the sake of this chapter let me simply say that we must be willing to move when God tells us to—otherwise we will miss the miracle. Mary simply said, "I am yours, God; do with my life what You will."

Where can you see God's favor and blessing upon you today? What has He made you especially good at? Don't tell me you are not good at anything, because I don't believe that for even a minute. Remember, the thing that made Mary special was the hand of God on her life. That is what makes you special too. Another word for

> THE THING THAT MADE MARY SPECIAL WAS THE HAND OF GOD ON HER LIFE.

favored is advantaged, and another word for blessed is happy.

So what are you advantaged at, and what makes you truly happy? Most importantly, how can you use that for God's glory? Mary was nurturing and loving, so much so that when God was going to send His Son to earth, God sent Him to Mary because He knew she would care for Jesus better than anyone else out there. Being nurturing and loving are not things that are going to land your name in lights, but they may very well be the simple tasks God has penciled next to your name on His great outline—they were what He penciled next to Mary's.

Proverbs 18:16 says, "A man's gift makes room for him and brings him before great men." What is your gift, and how can you see it making room for you somewhere? Proverbs 22:29 says, "Do you see a man skilled in his work? He will stand before kings; he will not stand before obscure men." God has big dreams for His daughters.

Remember, the only thing little about your life is how little you let God use it. When you give it over fully to God, there is no limit to what He can do. Don't miss the miracle that is on its way to you today because you don't understand it. Embrace your gift (or gifts), step forward, and let God use you. Be a history maker like Mary was.

When I imagine Mary at the end of her life (here goes my vivid imagination again), I see a few brown streaks woven throughout her now gray hair. Her eyes are tired, and her wrinkles make deep creases around her mouth and just beneath her eyes. I can see her rocking back and forth in a handcrafted wooden chair made for her by her Son—her Son she only had with her for a mere thirty-three years.

Her husband was gone by then too, and Mary was left alone. But on this particular afternoon, the one I am picturing in my mind, the Nazareth sun is offering a warm glow to the quickly darkening sky. Thinking of Jesus' promise that He went to prepare a place for her, she pauses for a moment of reflection. *It's almost time to go home*, Mary thinks, *and once again I will get to see Jesus.* Suddenly her mind is filled with snapshots playing out like a favorite home movie.

She can see Jesus on the day He came into the world

as she cradled Him in her arms. She can see Him as a pudgy toddler giggling with glee as He runs into her arms for a hug. She can see Him as He grew from a boy into a man and became less concerned with doing His chores and more interested in saving men's souls. And she can see Him in agony as He hung on the cross. Tears still sting her eyes as she thinks of that day. But Mary also sees Jesus as He was the last time she saw Him—radiant at His ascension. He was going home, and suddenly Mary's heart was filled with delight.

Yes, Mary thought as she watched the setting sun, *Gabriel was right. I am the most blessed of all women. For some reason God did favor me. I have lived a truly full life.*

Mary did not know, on the fateful day Gabriel visited her, all that God would do with her life or require of her in the process. She just knew she was favored and blessed—she took God at His word and stepped into the realm of the miraculous. Only later on, when she would evaluate her life in hindsight, would she see how all of the pieces fit.

Mary lived a full life by accepting what it meant to be favored and blessed, and by rising to the task of a lifetime—one that wasn't always easy, but certainly proved to be worth it in the end. She signed up for a lifelong adventure when she was just a girl. Are you willing to do the same?

2

TROUBLED BY QUESTIONS

"But [Mary] was very perplexed at this
statement, and kept pondering what kind of
salutation this was.... Mary said to the
angel, 'How can this be, since
I am a virgin?'"
—Luke 1:29, 34

We sat on my dorm room floor cross-legged, hair wadded up on our heads, and an open bag of candy between us, having one of our regular late-night "meaning of life" chats. I met Lindsay my freshman year in college, and we remained friends all through our time at Biola. There were many deep and meaningful conversations over the years, but one sticks out more than the rest.

It was our sophomore year, and I was struggling with finding God's will for my life. With many options before me, I was completely confused (and freaked out) by the thought of selecting one path and traveling it for the remainder of my life.

I am a person who likes tangible and definite answers—not Christian clichés or abstract concepts.

Repeatedly I asked Lindsay how you know if something is God's will or not.

Although I don't remember all the details of our conversation that night, I pelted her with countless "What if . . ." questions. Gesturing at me with a handful of M&M's, her sloppy bun bounced as she vigorously nodded and answered my questions. Finally, Lindsay said, "God hasn't given you the events of your life to hold in your own hands. He is allowing you to watch them unfold in His."

OUR STRUGGLES WITH GOD ARE USUALLY ABOUT ONE THING: CONTROL.

I know our conversation continued long after that statement, but that was all I needed to hear. Yes, I was troubled by questions, but the answers weren't up to me.

My real problem wasn't about what I was or wasn't supposed to do with my life. It was that I wasn't in control, and I wanted to be. In that late night conversation I began to understand that the questions we let trouble us are nothing more than a failure to trust God.

Demanding answers from heaven is simply our way of wrestling with God for control of our lives. Yes, sometimes we need to seek wisdom and guidance in choosing a direction. But most of the time we ask questions we *want* answers to, not questions we *need* answers to in that moment.

Our struggles with God—no matter what they are

centered around—are usually about one thing: control. If God is in control, then we are not, and that tends to bother us when our circumstances are not how we would have them be if we were the ones in charge. What we don't realize in the heat of the moment is there is only a struggle because we are fighting God.

If we choose to stop fighting and surrender control (which we don't have anyway), we will realize that God's plan is perfect and He is far more qualified than we are to orchestrate the events of our lives. After all, He is the creator of absolutely everything.

We don't want to wait for God to reveal His plan for our lives to us in *His* timing; we want to pray "microwave" prayers that produce something we can instantly feast on. But most of God's greatest blessings are only rich because they have been seasoned with the passage of time—lessons learned in God's silence.

If we completely trust God with the events and people in our lives, we will not be troubled by anything— even questions God sees fit to leave unanswered. In the months and years following my conversation with Lindsay, God did not give me direct answers to the questions that plagued my mind that night. The answers came over time as He unfolded His plan through my circumstances.

He answered Mary in much the same manner. There she was, completely startled by Gabriel's appearance in her living room (or whatever room she was in at the time of their encounter). She was troubled by the divine interruption in her life, and was unsure of what to think of the predicted outcome. How in the world was a virgin going to become pregnant—with the Son of God, no less?

I can just see her standing in the presence of Gabriel, brow wrinkled in confusion, mouth agape. She probably struggled to find words to formulate her question. Have you ever felt that way? I know I have had many moments where I felt like I needed to run and get a Q-tip and clean out my ears just to make sure I heard God right.

In the same way that God shocked Mary with His plans for her, He delights in surprising us with radical revelations and seemingly impossible plans that leave us standing in wonder—questioning if we heard Him correctly and sometimes even pondering whether or not it was God's voice we heard at all.

God graciously allowed Gabriel to answer Mary's first question—but I am sure there were many other questions that went unanswered in the months and years to come. And Gabriel's answer to Mary's first question was not even that helpful.

"The Holy Spirit will come upon you, and the power of the Most High will overshadow you; and for that reason the holy Child shall be called the Son of God," he said in Luke 1:35, as if that really answered what she asked.

If I were Mary, my next question would have been, "Okay, but *how* exactly is He going to do that? Will it hurt?" Perhaps it all happened so fast Mary was left speechless. Or maybe she was just naturally less inquisitive than most of us.

Whatever the cause may have been, we know God saw

fit to give one small girl one very large task. And He deemed it acceptable to leave many questions lingering in her mind as He unfolded His plans and accomplished what He promised.

PUZZLE PIECES THAT DON'T SEEM TO FIT

Imagine how Mary must have felt over the thirty years that followed Gabriel's announcement to her. When she went to visit Jesus as He was ministering, only to hear Him tell the crowd, "My mother and My brothers are these who hear the word of God and do it" (Luke 8:21), can't you just hear her heart breaking? She may have even felt betrayed in that moment. *Don't I mean anything to you, Jesus? God, why are you doing this to me? Have I not been faithful? What does that statement mean, anyway?* Many questions probably ran through her mind.

I don't know about you, but I think in a straight line. Structure and routine are my friends. People like me appreciate clearly defined outlines, itineraries, maps, and step-by-step instructions for assembling items that come in pieces. Puzzles frustrate me, and winding roads nauseate me. I plan everything in advance, and I have a tendency to overpack just in case I find myself needing the notorious kitchen sink when I am away from home. It might be just because of this that God delights so much in frustrating my own plans and schedules.

So many times I find myself examining the pieces of my life, wondering, *How in the world does all of this fit together?* Last weekend I went on a mother-daughter trip with my mom and some friends of ours. We rented a red convertible

Mustang (you can't get more fun than that), but when we met up we realized it would be next to impossible to fit the four of us—and all of our luggage—into that car.

Luckily my friend Rachel loves puzzles, and before long she had all of us, and all of our stuff, crammed into the convertible, and we were on our way. We were cramped, but we had a blast. My frustration was for no reason—just because I couldn't see how it would all fit didn't mean it wouldn't all fit.

Many times, frustration leads us to faith like nothing else can. Recently I attended a conference requiring air travel. I arrived at the airport early, just like the airline advised me to, but because of a security breach in a nearby terminal, the lines were extra long and I missed my flight.

I got a seat on a flight—four hours later—which put a big kink in *my* plans for the day, and I became distraught as I learned the airline could not locate my suitcase. The people at the ticket counter politely told me I would have to board the plane "having faith" that my luggage would somehow meet up with me on the other side.

As I sat on the plane looking out at the beautiful California coast below me, I thought of how that particular flight was a metaphor for my life. I had to get on board without knowing what kind of situation was waiting for me on the other end. Many times, God leads us down dimly lit paths where we are left merely guessing about what awaits us up ahead.

When I landed and eventually spotted my bag, I had never before been so excited to see my suitcase. But what about all the times when the suitcase doesn't arrive? What do we do when God shuts doors we thought He had opened for us? How do we deal with the uncertainty and apprehension that comes when He opens doors we never knew existed?

We have two choices—we can live in fear, or we can live in faith. There is no other choice, there is no in between. In his bestselling book *The Journey of Desire*, John Eldredge says, "The more comfortable you are with the mystery in the journey, the more rest you will know along the way."[1]

I am sure you have your own set of unanswered questions plaguing you. Perhaps you are wondering where you are to go to college, why your boyfriend broke up with you, why your parents got divorced, or why someone you love had to die. Maybe you are questioning whether or not you should apply for a certain job or go on a specific missions trip.

No matter what your questions are, you can take refuge in verses like Jeremiah 33:3, which says, " 'Call to Me and I will answer you, and I will tell you great and mighty things, which you do not know.' " But what do we do when God's answer comes in the form of silence? What do we do when God tells us the opposite of what our circumstances seem to scream? How do we respond when the things we were counting on don't work out?

It is in moments of heartache and confusion we need to remind ourselves that God did not promise to give us audible answers—sometimes His answers lie hidden in the midst of the very circumstance that is bringing us grief or stress. Those answers can only be uncovered by those with faithful hearts who are going to *choose* to look for the hand of God in everything.

> "WHEN YOU CANNOT TRACE HIS HAND, YOU CAN ALWAYS TRUST HIS HEART."

In high school, my friend Elizabeth used to quote the lyric, "God is too wise to be mistaken. God is too good to be unkind. And, when you cannot trace His hand, you can always trust His heart."[2]

Perhaps you are having a hard time tracing His hand today. Maybe you cannot imagine anything better for you than the one thing God has chosen to withhold in this moment. That's when we need to remind ourselves that we live with a limited perspective.

We can cross our arms and stomp our feet and demand that God explain to us what He is doing (which He most likely will *not* do, no matter how big a tantrum we throw) or we can step forward in faith like Mary did, and say, "Lord, I don't understand why or how—but I'll go where You lead me anyway."

WHY GOD FRUSTRATES OUR PLANS

When God frustrates our plans and itineraries, it is usually for one of two reasons. Sometimes it is to *protect us from danger*, like when we miss a plane that later crashes, or when we are stuck in traffic that prevents us from being at a certain intersection when an accident occurs. Danger is not always about life or death either; sometimes the danger He is protecting us from is dating the wrong person, accepting the wrong job, or going on the wrong missions trip. You cannot be in the right place or with the right person if you are in the wrong place or with the wrong person.

Because God has given us a free will, He has granted us the freedom to make mistakes that will keep us from His perfect plans for our lives. It's been said, "God will not do by miracle what I am to do by obedience." That means when heaven is silent, it is in our best interest not to move. We should not try to create our own answers when God refuses to reveal His; doing so *always* creates a huge mess.

In Genesis 16–21 we find Abraham trying to fulfill God's promise for a son by sleeping with Hagar, his wife's maidservant. The end result was Ishmael, not Isaac. Although God took longer than Abraham wanted Him to, He still came through and provided the son of promise. But because of Abraham's hurried heart, Ishmael was born, and from his seed the nation of Islam was created. We are still reaping the consequences of Abraham's mistake to this day!

Sometimes, though, God intervenes in our lives in a way that merits many questions but produces no answers because *He wants to reveal His plan to us by a change in our pace or a change in our path.* For Mary, God sent Gabriel to interrupt her plans in order to place her on a path she never dreamed of taking. She went from being a random girl in the middle of nowhere to being the mother of the Messiah.

God has changed my pace many times. Being a visionary person, God has often had to slow me down in order to prevent me from running ahead of His schedule. Sometimes, though, He quickens my pace—like when He had me take advanced placement classes in high school. Those classes later allowed me to graduate from college a semester early so I could step into a ministry I had no idea about back when I was taking the classes. Speeding me up when I was eighteen kept me on track when I was twenty-one.

Both the slowing and quickening of our steps are ordained by God to ensure we are led to the right place at the right time according to God's great plan. God chooses to take us down paths we do not understand by ways we do not know because He cares that much about building our character. Can you believe that? It blows my mind how much He cares about shaping our character and making us more like Him.

It's been said that who we are in our current surroundings is who we will be in our desired surroundings. Good thing God cares about preparing us, otherwise we probably would not be ready for the tasks He has ahead. He had to build faith in Mary on the day she first heard Jesus was coming so that she would be able to remain faithful and hopeful years later—when Jesus was lying in a tomb and it looked as if all God promised had failed.

Pastor David Jeremiah once said, "We build our faith by doing things that seem hard to us at the time so that we can gain strength to do the really hard things that come to us in the future."[3] That was true in Mary's life, and many times it is true in ours as well.

The situations in our lives all build on each other. It is not a series of many continuous journeys—it is one long journey with many twists and turns. Recently I had a crisis moment where I found myself banging on heaven's door, asking God if He was sure I was in the right spot. Things were not panning out at the pace, or in the way, I wanted them to. I looked at my situation and thought, *This can't be what God promised. I must have missed a turn somewhere.*

Ironically, a few weeks later I met an older gentleman named John, who works with high school students in his neighborhood. When he found out I wrote and spoke to teens, he was interested in hearing about my ministry. Through the course of our conversation he said something that struck a chord deep within me.

"It's so great you know where you are going at such a young age," he said, and then corrected himself. "Or at least you know Whom you are following." With the second half of his statement, John unknowingly gave me the precise word of encouragement I needed to keep going. The truth was, I *didn't* know where I was going. In all reality, I still don't. But I do know Whom I am following, and that makes all the difference.

Some of the questions we have will never be answered on this side of heaven. Others will be answered months and years after we first ask them, when God can unfold the circumstances and explain the reasons why. And still others will be answered immediately, as if God were just waiting for us to ask them.

No matter when our answers come, God is always at work behind the scenes orchestrating the events of our lives. He always has our best interest in mind, even when it doesn't seem like it at the time.

It is in moments of unanswered questions we need to practice patience in our lives. Someone once told me never to ask God to give me patience, because then everything would go wrong so that He could teach me what it means to be truly patient. But patience is a virtue we all need to cultivate in our lives.

God will work as He pleases whether we give Him permission to or not. But in the times when we do give Him permission to frustrate *our* plans or work without giving us an explanation, we can experience true freedom that only comes from trusting God completely.

LEARNING TO TRUST

Romans 8:28 says, "And we know that God causes all things to work together for good to those who love God, to those who are called according to His purpose." There is no maybe in that sentence—we *know* without a shadow of a doubt God causes *all* things to work together for our good. Even the bad things. Even the unexplainable things. Even the things that trouble us.

Sometimes we have a hard time understanding that because we don't see the whole picture. We can't see why God is withholding the answer, so we have to blindly go forward in faith, believing that in the end God will have accomplished the best thing for us.

In the end it always comes around. God always comes

through. On the day Jesus rose from the dead, Mary's heart must have experienced peace and rest unlike any peace and rest she had ever known in her lifetime. God finally pulled back the skies and showed her heaven. Understanding probably mixed with gratitude as she saw the magnitude of what she had been a part of, and the purpose behind all of her pain became clear.

God could not have explained it all to her in the beginning—she wouldn't have understood. He had to give her His plan for her life slowly over time so she could come to know Him in an intimate and special way as she began to understand what God was doing in her life.

And so it is with you. God is choosing to withhold some of the answers you are seeking at this time in your life because He wants to teach your heart to trust Him. More than anything else in this world, God desires a deep and intimate relationship with you. That was the purpose of sending Jesus. He will go to great lengths to get your attention. Sometimes the only way He can is to prove to you that you can't do it without Him. Sometimes God has to teach us how much we need Him in order to teach our hearts to truly love Him. The best way to do this is to show us that we are not in control.

Sometimes, in my quiet times with God, I just sit down, listen, and write down what I hear Him saying deep in my heart as a way of holding on to His words. Years ago, around the same time Lindsay and I had the memorable conversation that opened this chapter, I wrote down what God was showing me at that time, and it has proven to be true many times. In His gentle whisper He said:

> *I have heard all of your requests. Believe it or not, you are not a lost cause. You have a hope set before you that is unimaginable. You have paths of joy stretched before you longer than meets the eye. But first, you must trust Me. I will take you down paths that will frustrate you, I will introduce you to people who will make you mad, I will tie your hands and allow you to struggle so you may see I take care of my own. I will walk into the fire with you and you will not be burned, I will part the sea blocking your path, I will send you manna when you are hungry and light when it is dark. When My face is hidden from you, I will pass by so you may see My shoulder as Moses did. And finally, when you are still with Me in brokenness, when I have appeared to do nothing and you have done nothing but wait in return ... then child, I will bless you. Then you will say, "Lo and behold, I have made it to the land of rainbows. Surely my God has not forgotten me!"*

What God spoke to me that night is true for all of us. God will usher each of us into the Promised Land in due time. He will one day illuminate our paths with His light so that we can see the answers to all the questions we have asked and all the things our hearts have longed for—but first we must come to trust Him for those answers. And we need to remember with gratitude all the times He didn't have to answer us but He chose to anyway.

Our attitude toward God needs to be that of former U.N. Secretary General Dag Hammarskjöld, who said: "For all that has been—thanks! For all that shall be—yes!"[4] We need to be willing to say yes to God even when

He meets our questions with silence or seemingly un-favorable answers.

We need to trust God when the way is unclear, the reasons are unexplained, and we absolutely cannot trace His hand no matter how hard we try. For it is in the very moments where we have the least control that God has the most control and is at work in our lives in ways we could never imagine or dream.

Just look at Mary—she lived a life filled with un-answered questions as she watched her son grow into the Savior He came here to be. The end result for Mary was a glorious revelation that could only be experienced after many years of waiting, wondering, and trying to put all of the pieces together.

In God's time, your unan-swered questions will be answered in much the same way. Perhaps your period of waiting is God's way of showing you He doesn't want you to seek answers—He wants you to seek Him. That slight change may be all it takes to open the mouth of God. Maybe you have been so busy listening for Him to say what you want to hear that you cannot hear what He is actually saying.

> HE DOESN'T WANT YOU TO SEEK ANSWERS—HE WANTS YOU TO SEEK HIM.

God wants us to put our faith in Him, not in answers to the questions that plague us. He wants to make you a girl with an all-or-nothing faith—a faith that gives every-thing it's got even when the way is not clear and the outcome is unknown. Mary had that kind of faith. She had faith in an unchanging God in the midst of the painful, ever-changing, and sometimes confusing situations in her life.

What kind of faith do you have today—the kind that demands answers or the kind that silently waits in the presence of God until the path becomes clear and the way is made known? One will leave you restless. The other will leave you rested.

The choice is up to you. Now is the time to decide. What's it going to be?

3

SURRENDERED OBEDIENCE

"Then Mary said, 'Behold the maidservant
of the Lord! Let it be to me
according to your word.'"
—Luke 1:38 (NKJV)

Harlot! The word probably rang through Mary's soul
with such force she involuntarily shivered. She wasn't one;
in fact, she couldn't have been further from one. But that
is not what other people would think. I can see her running her hands through her long dark hair and straight-
ening her headpiece, trying to calm her nerves. *Did he really*
say I would be with child—God's child?

I envision Mary backing herself into a chair, running
her hand down her face—not in disbelief, but in shock at
what just occurred. God knocked on her door, and she
answered. She didn't really think about it; her decision
came naturally, almost as if instinct took over where emotion went numb.

Once Gabriel left her presence, she had time to sit
and ponder the things she had just experienced. In a few
months her belly would bulge and all of Nazareth would

know that she—this girl with the child growing inside of her—was not married. The world was under the impression that there was only one way to make a baby. Only Mary and God knew there were really two.

Yes, the Jews had been looking for their Messiah for years, but they would never believe He would come through the womb of a poor girl from a low-class town. No, the King of the world would not be born into poverty. Common sense said there was no way. Ah, but Gabriel said something different, and he was sent from God.

When Gabriel returned from his mission and entered the great throne room, God was most likely smiling.

"That was easy," I can see Gabriel saying after kneeling in God's presence.

God would nod in agreement. "I told you I picked the right girl—she didn't hesitate for even a minute."

The penalty in those days for premarital pregnancy was to be stoned to death. Mary knew that when she agreed to be part of God's plan. What we most often fail to realize is that Mary had a choice in this whole matter. Gabriel's words to Mary did not come in the form of a command; she had to agree to the divine offer. Mary submitted to the will of God out of obedience *and* out of her own free will.

She could have said no. She could have scoffed at the offer or cowered in fear. She could have told Gabriel she would pray about it and he needed to come back later. But Mary did none of those things. Mary said yes.

Now, I am not saying we should always instantly say

yes to all ministry opportunities that arise. Some matters require prayerful consideration before decisions can be made. But other times there is no question—God is in it, and we need to act.

Mary was asked to relinquish her reputation, her honor, and her very life if she needed to in order to answer God's call. Think about that for a second. Mary—who was a virgin—was asked to take on a role that would cause many to think of her as loose in her morals and worthy of death. Insults would fly every time she stepped outside, and the baby—after He was born—would be forced to endure accusations that He was illegitimate.

Would you relinquish your reputation, your honor, and your life to answer the call of God? Many of us flinch when God requires something far smaller from us. The following words once fell from the pen of missionary Amy Carmichael, who was another young woman God used to do great things: "If there be any reserve in my giving to Him who so loved that He gave His Dearest for me; if there be a secret 'but' in my prayer, 'Anything but *that*, Lord,' then I know nothing of Calvary love."[1]

What do you know of Calvary love? Calvary (Jesus' crucifixion) had not even happened yet, and Mary held nothing back when it came to what she was willing to give her Lord. Should any less be expected of us?

Mary knew she would be misunderstood, she knew she would be scorned and scoffed at in her own town, she knew Joseph might choose to turn his back on her, and she knew she might have to die because of what she was willing to do for God. Think of that—Mary was willing to die for God before she ever knew He was sending His Son to die for her. What a testimony of faithfulness. How many of us would have done the same?

Had they known about her call, even some of those who knew Mary best might have been surprised by the boldness and faithfulness expressed by her that day. One commentary described Mary as an illiterate young girl between the ages of twelve and fourteen, with nothing going for her: "She was too young to know much of the world or to have accomplished anything."[2] Bottom line: nobody expected much of Mary—nobody but God, that is. He wasn't surprised by her faithful response to Him that fateful day.

Mary's response to God's call should stand as a perfect example for those of us who are seeking to obey God in our lives today. She didn't know all that His plan would entail; she didn't know how He would pull it off; she didn't know what would become of her in the process. She only knew what it would cost her to obey, and she didn't waver for even a minute. She couldn't foresee all the blessings—she could only see the bottom line. Often, it is the same with us.

RESPONDING TO HIS CALL

When I was sixteen, I had only a vague idea of what God wanted me to do with my life. (Sometimes I still feel as if I only have a vague idea.) I read the biographies of several great men and women of faith and was inspired by their stories. I saw something in their lives I wanted. There was something about being abandoned to God that seemed exciting, but there was also something about it that seemed scary.

Being only a high school student, I wasn't sure what I could give. And I wasn't sure if I would want to, once I found out what it was God was asking of me. So I prayed and pondered, asking God what it was He wanted. As I did, these words fell from my pen onto the page of my journal:

If He gave us His all on that cross, and He gave us life through death, how can we ever give Him—the lover of our souls—anything less than all we have to give? He asks all because He gave all; He gave all because He loves all. He asks

> ## HE ASKS ALL BECAUSE HE GAVE ALL.

because He loves, and we must give in hopes that we may someday love too.

Slowly I began to realize that loving God meant sacrifice. I didn't feel called to the jungles of Africa or to the orphanages in Mexico, like others I knew. But I did feel called to serve in youth ministry at my church and to make a stand for Christ on my public school campus. Sure, they were seemingly small things, but I jumped into those commitments wholeheartedly.

During my high school career there was a period of time when I became very ill and doctors did not immediately know what was wrong. After a series of abnormal test results, they rushed me into surgery, unsure of what they would find. As my small frame shook with fear on a hospital gurney, somewhere across town a teacher at my high school—who was notorious for her loose lifestyle—

put her job on the line when she asked the students in my first-period class to stand, join hands, and pray for me because I believed in God and I believed in prayer. Later on, I was healed of my ailment and that teacher came to Christ.

Both students and teachers were taking notice of the difference in my life, and lives were changing. Small task, yes—but it brought huge results. I didn't even have to do anything radical; I just had to be me, and God did the rest.

As I answered God's call to be in the world but not of it, I also answered His call to mentor and encourage those who were younger than me. As a high school student I began to disciple junior high students in my church. Years later, after I went off to college and they went into high school, several of them rose up to disciple younger generations too. It was a chain reaction; the people I touched were out there touching other people. My all wasn't much in my own eyes, but God saw what He could turn it into. So He asked me to give Him my life, and with it He changed the lives of those around me.

Who are you touching today? Think of those who have influenced your life for Christ. Have you told them how much they inspired you? Now may be the time to jot that note, send that e-mail, or make that phone call. Your words might be just what those people need to keep encouraging others and to continue pressing on.

How about those younger than you—is there someone whose life you could build into? Maybe there's someone in your sphere of influence who could use a smile and a quick hug today. Sometimes the littlest things spark the greatest changes.

FINDING THE COURAGE TO STAND

My task wasn't anything like Mary's, but I was still afraid when God asked me to step out. I took ridicule from popular kids at my high school. Even some people at church told me I was in the wrong ministry, that I was wasting my time on kids who would not listen. The dirty looks I got from some of the kids in the hallway at school were probably only slightly less harsh than the dirty looks Mary got from those who judged her as "cheap" and "easy."

> SOMETIMES THE LITTLEST THINGS SPARK THE GREATEST CHANGES.

Other people may not—and probably will not—understand the call that God has on your life. Sometimes you will be asked to do things that seem crazy to other people, and you will be asked to put your all out there on the line. Just look at Mary. She had nothing going for her in the deal she made with God—except a promise no one could see but her.

In college I met a girl who was an exchange student from Korea. She had a thick accent, and sometimes it was hard for people to understand her. With tears flowing down her cheeks one afternoon, she told our class about the struggles she was facing in the United States and how heartbreaking it was to be misunderstood—especially in the church. Her words were broken, and because of her culture she worshiped God in a somewhat different style from the rest of us. Sometimes other Christians wondered if she was serving the same God they were, questioning her motives. She went under the fire of persecution in much the same way Mary did.

Have you ever experienced a "language barrier" as you set out to serve God? Have those around you ever questioned your heart and your ability to hear God because they didn't understand the work He was doing in and through you? Rest assured, you are not alone. Mary and my dear friend from school were misunderstood too.

But both of them lived in such a way, and loved God in such a way, that over time it was impossible to question their motives. Their love for God was evident in their actions. How evident is your love for God? My friend Todd used to say, "If being a Christian were a crime, would there be enough evidence in your life to convict you?"

Often, when God calls us to rise to great tasks, He asks us to empty our hands of all we are holding. He asks us to be willing to be misunderstood. God does this so He can bless us with a rich abundance as we serve Him. Only when we are empty of ourselves can we be filled with Him. But it is up to us to decide whether we are willing to take the risks and obey at all costs.

What it costs us to step up and answer God's call on our lives is incidental. What really matters is that we heed the call when it comes to us with a quick and simple yes, just like Mary did. After all, 1 Samuel 15:22 tells us that to obey is better than sacrifice in the eyes of God.

Many of us have heard the story of Esther. She has even risen to a new level of popularity, with countless books and movies telling the story of her life. Her motto was "For such a time as this..."

If I could give Mary a motto, it would be "For such a task as this..." I know it's similar to Esther's motto, and many people would say it means the same thing. But when I look at these two girls I see their stories moving in the same direction. One was exalted to royalty; the other gave birth to royalty. Both girls were key players in saving God's people. Neither had within themselves the power to save. But in the hands of God both women became powerful tools and each played a defining role in her generation.

TRACES OF MARY TODAY

But what about *our* generation? Both the times and the tasks are calling for girls who are willing to stand up and change our world. Years ago there were countless girls dedicating their lives to the Lord. Two who stand out in my mind are Elisabeth Elliot and Catherine Marshall. In college they both developed into girls in the line of Mary. Both of their biographies have inspired me to pursue God in a more passionate way.

As a high school student I used to read about Catherine and Elisabeth's days at college, and I could see them sitting in their dorm rooms writing journal entries and prayers that would later serve as landmarks in their spiritual journeys. Elisabeth even left behind a man she loved and ventured off to the mission field. Her book, *Passion and Purity*, tells that story.

I eagerly wanted to follow in their footsteps. I went to a Christian college, hoping to meet other girls who wanted to do the same. But by the time I got to college, I found myself looking around and wondering where the Elisabeths and Catherines had gone. Don't get me wrong, there were many faithful girls who loved and served God. But after close examination it was evident that some of the passion that Elisabeth and Catherine had was missing from my generation.

It seems to me there is a new kind of girl taking over the world; she is even taking over the Christian world. She is modern and independent, focused on glittering up her outside, and has forgotten how to tend to her inward life. Now, this is not a new phenomenon. Even in her spiritual autobiography, *Meeting God at Every Turn*, Catherine Marshall describes her wealthy roommate at Agnes Scott College.

Her name was Virginia and she had the finest clothes, an endless supply of makeup, and was a real live "blond bombshell." And there sat her roommate, plain old mousy-haired Catherine, writing things in her journal about how she wanted to know and seek God more, so she could find His purpose for her life. Today, it seems there are many Virginias and few Catherines. Far too many girls are saying no to God and yes to the world. There are barely any traces of Mary in this current generation.

She was wide-eyed that day, but disobedience was out

of the question. Turning God down wasn't even a thought. Yes, Mary was all smiles as she willingly submitted to what God was asking. She was like the woman described in Proverbs 31:25: "Strength and dignity are her clothing, and she smiles at the future."

Mary brought new meaning to the word *independence*, because she was willing to truly stand alone—without Joseph, without her family, without the support of her small town. But she also balanced that independence with the perfect amount of dependence. She knew what it meant to take refuge in God.

> MARY BROUGHT NEW MEANING TO THE WORD *INDEPENDENCE.*

Mary also gave new meaning to the word *trust.* She asked only one question when Gabriel appeared to her with God's message: How? And when he answered her, she fell silent, gave a slight nod, and stepped into the realm of the impossible.

"God will take care of me," I can hear Mary whisper to herself months later as she rubbed her hand over her protruding belly and wandered through her house. And God did.

God will take care of you too. He will go to great lengths to bring His purposes about, as His eyes scour the earth in search of the faithful. Imagine that—God has looked through all time, He has sifted through all nations, He has thumbed through the pages of the lives of everyone you know, and those you don't, and He has assigned a task to you that *only you* can fulfill. Out of all those people, He wants *you* for the job because He thinks you are perfect for it.

ROCK YOUR WORLD!

Sometimes God draws our attention to things that aren't getting done—not so that we can complain, but so we can get in there and get things done ourselves. When I was in high school our youth group hit some rough times. There were no leaders to help our youth pastor, and there were no events or Bible studies to attend outside of the Sunday service, the midweek study, and an annual church camp.

There was a group of us who regularly prayed that this would change. But when the situation didn't, God showed us that He wanted us to *be* the change in the situation. So we went to our youth pastor and proposed a game plan—and the Girl's Getaway summer outing was formed. We found a cabin, picked a theme, rented a bus, bought a bunch of food, and divided the topics up into different Bible studies we would teach to our peers.

Our planning committee met for weeks. We bathed this weekend retreat in prayer for months. On the day it all kicked off, some of us showed up early to decorate the cabin and make sure the gifts we made for those who attended were ready to be given out. There were pictures on the walls, decorations all over the tables, and the smell of dinner was in the air when the girls arrived. It was a weekend to remember—and remembered it was.

The turnout was so great we had to turn girls away before sign-ups were even finished. The cabin we rented could only sleep forty, and there were more girls than beds. The theme for the weekend was radical relationships, and God really met us in a unique way. Several girls came to Christ and others recommitted their lives to Him. It was an awesome weekend that changed girls; it especially changed the lives of those of us who planned it and put it together.

Our newly formed leadership team designed the weekend in such a way that everyone used her strength to bring the team to its fullest potential. Kelly came from a big family, so she taught on family relationships. Ruby had learned a few recent lessons about how to date (and how not to date), so she taught on guy-girl relationships. Gina had been digging into the meaning of friendship, so she taught on being a true friend. And that weekend I had the privilege of teaching on the importance of our relationship with Christ.

After the main sessions, the girls broke into discussion groups led by other peer leaders on our planning team. People really opened up and bonded through sharing their struggles and similarities. Girls who were life-long acquaintances went home as friends. Others went home and mended rifts with siblings and parents. It was awesome, and it didn't stop there.

After we got down from our "mountaintop experience," we started weekly home Bible studies and discipleship groups. There were no leaders for our youth group so God raised some of us up to lead the others.

Don't let the fact that you are young discourage you. Use it to your advantage. You can say and do a lot of things with your peers that those who are older than you can't.

If age is something that tends to get you down, write out 1 Timothy 4:11–12 and stick it somewhere you will see it—like maybe on your bathroom mirror so you see it every morning as you are getting ready to face your day. It has inspired me many times. I especially love *The Message* translation: "Get the word out. Teach all these things. And don't let anyone put you down because you're young. Teach believers with your life: by word, by demeanor, by love, by faith, by integrity."

Live God's Word out in your actions. Let it be seen and heard in the things you say, in the way you behave and react, in your attitude toward others, in your ability to step out on a limb when God asks you to, in your ability to trust God when it doesn't make sense, and by living out a lifestyle marked by a purity that never compromises.

We all have different talents, abilities, and callings, but we are all called to rock our world for Jesus Christ. Each of us is to stand up and make a difference—no matter what it costs us. God wants us to find the things that are not being done and then get in there and get them done. He doesn't send Gabriel down with individual messages for His daughters anymore, but He does make His will known. Perhaps you know what it is you should be doing but have been putting it off because you are unsure of how to go about it or you are scared.

Remember—the God who calls always equips. Take a step of faith like Mary. Say something simple like, *Okay*

God. I'm here and I'll do it. If you mean it from your heart, all of the resources of heaven will be at your disposal to make sure you get the job done.

Maybe you don't know what you are called to do and this whole concept of God having a tailor-made task just for you is all a little new. Then hit your knees and start praying. Read God's Word, look at how God has gifted you, and try to figure out how you can use your passions for His glory. Be a willing vessel. Mary was, and that was all it took for God to unleash a miracle.

Perhaps you know what you are supposed to be doing, and like Mary you have risen to meet your call. Good for you! Keep it up. Stay in the Word and stay on your knees. When you enter heaven's royal throne room someday you will hear the coveted words, "Well done, good and faithful servant. Enter into the joy of your lord" (Matthew 25:21 NKJV).

The clock has been set and the task has been assigned. Today is the day to decide: Are you going to answer God's call with a yes or are you going to tell Him to come back later? Maybe there won't be a later. But whether there is or not isn't the point. Delayed obedience is really just disobedience in another form.

A simple yes from the mouth of Mary was all it took for God to send a Savior to the world. There is no telling what a simple yes from your mouth will do today.

4

AN OVERFLOWING HEART

"And Mary said: 'My soul exalts the Lord,
and my spirit has rejoiced in God my Savior.
For He has had regard for the humble state of
His bondslave; for behold, from this time on
all generations will count me blessed.'"
—Luke 1:46–48

When I was in high school my youth group hosted monthly nights of worship and communion in students' homes. For a while we met at mine. On a certain date each month my living room would be packed with about forty high schoolers crammed into the small space like a bunch of sardines.

People sat elbow to elbow and knee to knee, but when the music started no one seemed to notice. The entire room was engulfed in worship. We were lost in the lyrics as we basked in the presence of God.

These monthly periods of worship were not enough for most of us. In the summer we had bonfires and nights of worship at the beach on almost a weekly basis. Back then worship was a lifestyle, and you could see the fruit of it in our lives. Our souls craved God, and we longed to praise Him all the time. We just couldn't get enough of Him.

I can't remember exactly when these nights of worship stopped, but somewhere along the way they got lost in the shuffle of school, work, and hanging out. When I was in college my dorm floor had weekly nights of worship; regrettably, I only made it out to them a few times.

Our university even had Sunday nights set aside for an optional time of worship in one of the chapels on campus. The number in attendance always dwindled as the semester wore on and people became busier. Sadly, the numbers were never as high at "Singspiration" as they were at our biannual "Get Your Roommate a Date" nights. Somewhere along the line, life just got too busy and something had to go. For some reason I was under the impression that worship was something you did *when you had time*. Mary's story showed me I was wrong.

Like my friends and I used to cram into my living room and sing our hearts out to God, Mary sang her heart out to Him as well. Only hers was a unique and original song. Called "The Magnificat" (taken from the Latin word *magnifies*), it is found in Luke 1:46–55, and it tells us more about Mary's life and heart than the rest of her story combined. Let's take a look at it:

> My soul exalts the Lord, and my spirit has rejoiced in
> God my Savior.
> For He has had regard for the humble state of His
> bondslave;

For behold, from this time on all generations will
count me blessed.

For the Mighty One has done great things for me; and
holy is His name.

AND HIS MERCY IS UPON GENERATION AFTER
GENERATION TOWARD THOSE WHO FEAR HIM.

He has done mighty deeds with His arm;

He has scattered those who were proud in the
thoughts of their heart.

He has brought down rulers from their thrones,

And has exalted those who were humble.

HE HAS FILLED THE HUNGRY WITH GOOD THINGS;
and sent away the rich empty-handed.

He has given help to Israel His servant, in remembrance of His mercy, as He spoke to our fathers,
to Abraham and his descendants forever.

Earlier in the book I told you that Mary was most
likely illiterate, which to me makes her song truly amazing. There is so much packed into those few verses that it
is almost unbelievable. In this song Mary shows extensive
knowledge of the Scriptures. Not only does she prophet-
ically speak of abundant blessings under the reign of her
son (with the poor being lifted up and the hungry being
satisfied), but she also praises God for all that He will do
through Jesus: Israel will be helped and the promises of
Abraham fulfilled.

But what impresses me most about this girl—who
scholars say could not read and did not have her own
copy of the Scriptures—is how she was able to quote passages from Old Testament prophecies with such accuracy.

If Mary could not read, how on earth could she know these things? I've *read* these Old Testament passages and they are not that fresh in my own mind. I don't think I even knew them that well when I studied them for my Old Testament exams in college!

The only way Mary could have known God and His Word so well was by faithfully practicing the spiritual disciplines of prayer and Scripture memorization. She was a true worshiper in every sense of the word. Mary trained her ear and tuned her heart to hear the Word of God, and she committed those precious words to memory. She took her time with God seriously, and the result was a lifestyle of worship that poured forth in everything she did. Her song recorded in Luke 1 was an automatic response to what God was doing in her life. If you had a song, how would it sound right now?

Think about this for a second. If she could not read, in order to know these Old Testament prophecies and create this song, Mary would have had to intently pay attention during her weekly visits to the synagogue. Because, unless her father read the Scriptures to her during the week, the Sabbath would have been her only exposure to them. Imagine that—she had to memorize God's Word by *listening* to it. That's amazing. When was the last time you listened that closely in church?

On a recent visit with my grandpa, he asked me if I could recount the main points from the sermon I had heard the week before. After wracking my brain and scrounging up a few bleak details, I gave up in defeat. He was trying to prove that people today generally don't listen that well when they go to church. I sat silent for a minute and then began to unpack an exhortation we both heard a few weeks earlier, detail by detail. That message had really ministered to me, so I remembered it well.

Our conversation really got me thinking and left me wondering why so many of us turn our "selective memory" on when we go to church. If we judge sermons solely on how they fit into our current circumstances, we miss the nuggets of knowledge God has for us each week. I'm not saying it is wrong to have favorite speakers or messages, or to listen more closely to messages that seem tailor-made for us, but we should strive to leave church with at least one point to take home with us each week.

THE PRIORITY OF WORSHIP

Mary's story proves that worship is not something that happens when you *have* time for it; it's something that happens when you *make* time for it. The result is a natural outpouring of praise that comes from spending time with Jesus. Mary lived a life of undivided worship to God. Can we say the same about our lives today? When was the last time you praised God just because He is God? In Psalm 86:11 (NIV) the psalmist cries out, "Give me an undivided heart." When was the last time you prayed a prayer like that *and meant it?*

> WHEN WAS THE LAST TIME YOU PRAISED GOD JUST BECAUSE HE IS GOD?

Distraction seems to nag at our souls every time we

sit down to worship God, pray, or read our Bibles. We are so accustomed to doing one thing while thinking about another that we often fall short of living out real worship; instead, we settle for a cheap imitation. Worship isn't just everybody singing together on Sunday morning—it's a lifestyle that reflects who we really are in every circumstance of life.

When we truly come to know and understand who God is, it is impossible to have any reaction other than to fall on our faces before Him in awe. If your breath is not taken away when you ponder God's majesty, then you're missing something.

Recently I was at Hume Lake Christian Camp in the Sierra Nevada Mountains. One morning a friend and I woke up early and went for a walk. We decided to walk out to the end of the dock and spend some time praying together. As she and I knelt side by side, taking in the majestic beauty of all God created, I found myself thinking, *There are no words for this.* It was like being in a postcard, and I was in awe of who God was. The lake was still, the mountains in the distance were snow capped, and giant redwood trees stretched to the heavens all around me. That moment will stay with me for the rest of my life.

Take a look at the world around you. Look at the ocean; notice the amazing variety of trees and plants; marvel at the brilliance of the sun; look at the sky when thunder strikes and lightning flashes as the heavens pour forth rain. Look at the order in the universe. Take a moment to study your baby cousin, who has her own miniature set of fingers and toes complete with tiny fingernails. How can you not be impressed? How can our hearts not be moved to worship a God like that?

A Heart of Hurry

I reached a time in college when I was too tired to worship God. I was busier than I had ever been, and with what little time I had left all I wanted to do was sleep. One time, in a particularly lethargic slump, I walked into my friend Dan's office—he was our student body president at the time—and I plopped into the chair across from him, waiting for him to look up. I don't remember everything we talked about that time, but he did say one thing that struck me to the very core.

"Shannon," he said, "if I have learned anything, it's that you cannot truly love God if you have a heart of hurry." I blinked at him and thought about what he said for a moment. Then I went on the defense, claiming I loved God even though I was one of the busiest people I knew.

> "YOU CANNOT TRULY LOVE GOD IF YOU HAVE A HEART OF HURRY."

I don't remember if he answered me or not. I think he just surveyed my frazzled state and looked at me with raised eyebrows. I walked out of his office that night with something to think about—and I haven't been able to stop thinking about it since. Our failure to truly worship God can usually be traced back to one of two things: busyness or laziness. True worship is the result of finding balance—being spiritually disciplined.

Part of living out a lifestyle of worship is making room and time for God. The first thing we must do when cultivating a lifestyle of worship and praise like Mary's is eliminate busyness and hurry. In their book *TwentySomeone*, Craig Dunham and his former college roommate Doug Serven put it this way: "Our struggle is not as much a matter of time management as it is of priority management . . . we are only able to have one priority."[1] They go on to say our culture has really messed things up by pluralizing the word *priority,* causing us to think we can have more than one.

Having anything else as our priority and giving God whatever remains when we are through with everything else is like going on a date with a guy whose idea of buying you dinner is letting you eat the leftovers off his plate. I don't know about you, but I certainly would not go for that!

The night I left Dan's office my priority was definitely not what it should have been, and I was left wondering just what I was going to do with my heavy heart of hurry. How do we get from where we are—with our misplaced priority and our hurried hearts—to where Mary was, with an overflowing heart of praise?

The answer is easier said than done. We must decimate the distractions in our lives. Distractions are things that are not as important as loving God and spending time with Him on a regular basis. They are things we give more attention to than they deserve.

I am a very organized—and at times rigid—person. I operate best with a schedule. If I put it on my calendar it will happen. If I don't, other things usually get in the way of whatever I was supposed to do. Just ask my friends; some days I have to actually pencil in meals on my calendar or I will get so busy I forget to eat.

So for me, part of eliminating hurry comes from scheduling God into the first half hour of every morning. That's not the only time I spend with Him throughout the day—but it is my *priority time* with Him. In that half hour I pour out my heart in prayer, I read daily passages in several devotional books, I read several chapters in the Bible, and I draw strength for the day. To me that half hour is non-negotiable. And it doesn't always go for just a half hour. It's not like the clock hits 6:30 and I slam my Bible shut. I simply use that half hour as a guide to make sure I'm starting my day with my priority in the right place.

Unless I wake up to some type of crazy emergency, I know the first half hour of every day belongs exclusively to God. When the alarm goes off and I want to hit snooze, I simply remind myself I have a date with the Creator of the universe and I cannot be late. For me, this was a step that helped in my quest to rid myself of my heart of hurry. It helped strengthen my relationship with Christ, and it helped me cultivate a heart of worship. Getting into God's presence is the quickest way to grow a heart of worship in your life. Something about being with God just makes you want to praise Him.

Habits of Praise

In college I met with a small group on a regular basis. Each week we would share prayer requests and exchange prayer cards with someone else in the room. When it came time for us to share with the whole group, my friend Amy used to say, "You have to share at least one praise with your prayer requests. There is always something to be thankful for."

Sometimes the room would grumble as we thought long and hard about what we could praise God for. We wanted to talk about what we wanted and needed, not what we already had.

But Amy's chiding developed an attitude of praise among our whole group. Eventually we were so excited to share our praises with each other that we sometimes forgot to mention our prayer requests. I would challenge you to share at least one praise next time you are sharing your prayer requests—it makes a big difference in your attitude and your perspective. The truth is, if we kept a fair score, our praises would always outnumber our requests.

I think habits such as Bible reading, prayer, and Scripture memorization are often viewed by us as burdens because we do not always *feel* like doing them. I received an e-mail from a friend this week; she ended it by saying, "I have no desire to call out to God at all, so please pray for me if you think about it." Along with promising to pray for her, I encouraged my friend to pray for herself and not wait until she "felt like it" once again.

Relationship with God takes effort and discipline. You must make the time to meet with God or else your life will slowly begin to unravel, and eventually you will find it spinning out of control. My friend Todd used to tell me that if I was experiencing problems in any of my other relationships, they could always be traced back to my relationship with God. If we are not right with God, we cannot be right with anyone else. It all goes back to what we *choose* to make our priority.

Praise was Mary's initial response to Gabriel's visit to her. I don't think she had to make time for the Magnificat; I think it came as a natural response from Mary having made time for memorizing the Old Testament and praying. If we look at our lives and praise is not our natural response, then we need to do a little work—whether we feel like it or not. And if we can look at our lives and see praise coming as naturally to us as breathing, then I would venture to say that this comes from the effort we have put into our time with God. But that still doesn't give us an excuse to slack off.

RADIATING GOD'S GLORY

The second thing we need to do to cultivate a life of praise is eliminate laziness. Praise is a product of time. It's like that saying, "We have to take the time to make the time..." It has nothing to do with how much stuff we have or how long we have been a Christian.

Have you ever met someone who just overflowed with praise? Someone whose face radiated God's glory? Someone whom you would refer to as a friend of God? Chances are, they probably are not the richest person you know. In fact, they may have even had to face a few hard knocks in life.

In Exodus 32–34 we find Moses spending *forty* days on Mt. Sinai conversing with God. He comes down with the Ten Commandments, breaks the tablets in anger over

Israel's idolatry, and then treks back up the mountain to meet with God again. The second time he is up there God lets him see part of His glory. And Moses descends with a shining face. It is so bright he has to cover it with a veil because the people are afraid of him.

Have you ever radiated God's glory in such a way that people saw a difference in your life? It should be our heart's desire to know God the way Mary and Moses did—face-to-face, in depth. We should pursue God with a reckless abandon, refusing to make anyone or anything else our priority—because when this life is over all we will have is our relationship with Christ. The depth and the strength of that relationship depend on us. Jesus already gave all He has; what are we giving in return?

> WHEN THIS LIFE IS OVER ALL WE WILL HAVE IS OUR RELATIONSHIP WITH CHRIST.

Because worship is a lifestyle and not a single action, it can take many forms. For me, sitting at my computer and writing is a form of worship because it connects my soul to God in a way nothing else does. For others, singing, dancing, or playing sports is a type of worship. Being a sports fan, nothing excites me more than to see Christians start their game with a prayer or give credit to God when they do well.

After a victory in a 2003 post-season game, Boston Red Sox right fielder Trot Nixon was interviewed about his game-winning home run. "It wasn't me swinging the bat," he said on national television, "it was the Lord Jesus Christ."

Already a Red Sox fan, that statement made me root for the team all the more. That response seemed to come naturally to Trot; it was his finest hour, yet he viewed baseball as a way of giving God glory. Isn't that what worship is really about? His teammate Curt Schilling did the same thing after pitching a winning game in the 2004 World Series on a faulty ankle. Curt told the world that he was only able to succeed in God's strength.

The Magnificat was Mary's way of praising God for what He was doing in her life—He was bringing the Messiah to the world, and He was using Mary to do it. How are *you* praising God for what He is doing in *your* life right now? Are you leaving behind a legacy of praise like Mary did?

If you could monitor the busyness and the laziness factors in your life at this moment, how would you measure up? Would you need to move more toward clearing your schedule of mundane tasks or more toward filling your life with time spent with God? Perhaps you need to do a little of both.

The Lord is rejoicing over you at this very minute. As He looked down on Adam in the Garden of Eden and "saw all that He had made ... was very good" (Genesis 1:31), so He looks down on you too. His heart is full to the brim with love and affection for you. Have you dug into His Word lately to see just how deep that love goes?

In Luke 19:40 Jesus says if His people become silent the stones will cry out and praise God, because that is how good and magnificent He is. I don't know about you, but I most certainly don't want a bunch of boring rocks doing my job! I want the world to know I serve a mighty, valiant, strong, kind, and loving God who took my sin upon himself and went to the cross for me.

How about you? When it comes to worshiping God, who is going to be louder—you or that boulder in your backyard?

5

SHUT OUT

"And she gave birth to her firstborn son;
and she wrapped Him in cloths,
and laid Him in a manger,
because there was no room
for them in the inn."
—Luke 2:7

I will never forget that night as long as I live. In one fleeting moment everything I believed was put to the test, and the consequences could have been deadly. It was my senior year of high school, and most of my friends from youth group had already graduated and were off to college. I was hanging out with some friends from school—two who professed to be Christians and two who didn't. We planned to celebrate my friend Kim's (all the names in this account have been changed) eighteenth birthday with an all-girls slumber party, and we went out to dinner beforehand at our usual hangout.

I was at a place in life where I was tired of feeling alone, and I just wanted to fit in and have some fun before going off to college. Still holding firmly to my convictions, I began surrounding myself with people who lived their lives and measured their morals by a different standard. Without realizing it, I had stepped into a danger zone.

At dinner we ran into a hot guy from our rival high school; some of the girls I was with knew him, but I didn't. He plopped down at our table and invited us to a "raging party" going on at a house where the parents were gone for the weekend. Jotting the address on a napkin, he gave a wink to one of my friends and disappeared.

Nobody really seemed too excited about the invitation at first. These girls were pretty partied out, and I had made up my mind a long time ago never to attend a party like that. To me, it always seemed like inviting trouble. So the five of us piled into my friend Tina's Camry like a bunch of sardines and made our way to Melanie's so she could change out of her work clothes and get comfortable for our night of chick flicks and chocolate chip cookies.

But somewhere during the short drive home, the other girls began to change their minds about the party. One by one they started to express an interest in going. Nearly panicking in the middle of the backseat, I began to hold my breath and silently pray that God would get me out of what could quickly become an ugly situation.

At first my attempts to talk them out of going seemed successful. "Come on guys," I reasoned, "parties like this happen every weekend, but Kim is only turning eighteen once." Slowly they all nodded. By the time we pulled into Melanie's driveway, I was beginning to think I might actually win the debate. I was wrong.

When we went inside and waited for Melanie to change her clothes, the girls began to name off all the guys who would probably be at this party—and my grip on victory slowly slipped away. As I overheard Melanie in the other room telling her mom what a "goody-two-shoes" and "killjoy" I was, it became apparent to me; I was going to have to make a choice—and I was going to have to stand alone.

When they were all ready and started to pile back into the car, I stood in Melanie's driveway, watching the four of them giggle and fasten their seat belts. When I didn't get in, Tina—the one I was closest to—rolled down her window and called out, "What are you doing?"

I shuffled my feet and looked down. Taking a deep breath, I finally looked her in the eye and said, "I can respect your decision to go to this party tonight, so you need to respect my decision not to go. I'll see you guys later." I took a deep breath and put my hands behind my back so the other girls couldn't see I was trembling.

The week before, the senior class had voted on the most popular kids in our five-hundred-plus student class, and four of us girls had taken home titles. After being named "Friendliest" senior girl, I thought my popularity had finally been established. But my decision to not attend the raging party threatened all my dreams of remaining popular.

After a short and curt argument in Melanie's driveway, Tina took me home and they all headed off to a party that was broken up by the police less than an hour later. The following Monday—the day homecoming queen ballots were due—my "friends" removed my name from the ballot, symbolically removing me from their group. Just as there was no room for Mary in the inn, suddenly there wasn't a place for me and my convictions in the "in crowd" at my public high school. I was shut out.

THE HIGH COST OF MARY'S OBEDIENCE

Think of Mary and how she must have felt on the night she and Joseph rode into Bethlehem. First of all, I cannot imagine being nine months pregnant and riding on the back of a donkey. Having witnessed the pregnancies of a few close friends, I don't even know how you would hoist a pregnant woman onto a donkey in the first place! How miserable Mary must have been on that long ride— and then to find out there was no room for her at the inn. If I had been in Mary's shoes, that news would have been just about all it would have taken for me to rethink the whole obedience thing.

Here she was, faithfully serving God in spite of being looked upon disgracefully because of her "illegitimate" pregnancy ... hadn't she already suffered enough? Don't you think she had already paid more than her fair share of dues? I mean, when Esther answered God's call on her life she was sent to a palace, but Mary couldn't even find a place to sleep in a poor man's inn. What was God thinking?

Some people suggest that the full inn was a blessing in disguise because it allowed Mary to give birth in privacy. But after hearing several descriptions of where she had to give birth, I'm not so sure how much of a blessing it could have really been. Even with privacy as an advantage, giving birth where the animals did could not have been that pleasant.

Sometimes God seems to ask a lot of those of us who decide to wholeheartedly pursue His will for our lives. Most times we would not agree to what He was asking if we knew what it really entailed. Perhaps God is asking you to give up your comfort like Mary. Maybe He is asking you to surrender seeming popularity for a life of purity, like He asked of me. Whatever He is asking for at this moment may seem big—even huge—and a part of your heart may be wrestling with the idea of simply acting like you never heard the call in the first place.

But weighing the cost before you can see the end of the story isn't fair to God either. That's like saying we know everything He's doing on our behalf all of the time. And we know that isn't true. Let's take a little road trip down to Bethlehem and you'll see what I mean. On second thought, let's take it back even a step further and visit Mary in Nazareth when the feeling of being shut out first began.

Although we have no way of knowing what the actual conversation was on the day that Mary told Joseph she was going to have a baby, Matthew 1:19 does tell us a little bit about Joseph's reaction: "And Joseph her husband, being a righteous man and not wanting to disgrace her, planned to send her away secretly."

Joseph knew that he and Mary had never been together intimately (in fact he was not technically her husband yet, but Jewish law regarded betrothal to be as legally binding as marriage, even though there had not yet been a consummation of the relationship).[1] So Mary's pregnancy was seen by Joseph—and by all of those who would soon find out—as adultery, which at that time was punishable by death.[2]

It's hard to imagine a more heartbreaking scene. Mary turns to the man she had planned to spend the rest of her life with, to tell him of the great blessing God was bestowing on her, and he wants nothing to do with her.

Mary had to have known Joseph wouldn't take the news too well, because the whole thing sounded ridiculous. An angel appearing to a virgin and announcing she would become pregnant by the Holy Spirit would seem a little sketchy to someone who hadn't brushed up on the Isaiah 7 prophecy (which actually foretells that the Messiah will be born of a virgin).

Oddly enough, most commentaries declare Joseph a righteous man because he wanted a divorce (hence the words "send her away secretly"). He didn't want to have Mary stoned; some commentaries say this is evidence of Joseph's love for her.[3]

But think about how horrible that news must have seemed to Mary. Here she was, not even technically married yet, and she was going to be divorced (which was not common in those days, like it is today). She was going to be all alone raising a baby—despised by her neighbors, her family, and her beloved Joseph. In that moment she probably could not have felt more unloved and shut out. She was facing the ultimate rejection.

Holding Fast to Our Convictions

How many of us are firm in our convictions and are willing to hold fast to our beliefs—until some smooth-talking, good-looking guy comes along? For many of us, the thought of being loved—or even liked—by an attractive and popular guy is enough to make us think twice about our convictions.

> SHE PROBABLY COULD NOT HAVE FELT MORE UNLOVED AND SHUT OUT.

I've heard some pretty bad excuses over the years and I've even come up with some pretty lame ones myself.

Some common excuses for wanting (and basking in) attention from a good-looking guy who is bad news are: "Well, God is going to use me to lead this guy to Christ." Or, "I'm just dating him. It's not like we are getting married or anything." The list could go on for miles, but it doesn't change the facts—when the guy for you comes along, you won't have to make excuses or compromise your convictions.

And Mary didn't either. Matthew 1:20–23 tells us God came to Joseph in a dream informing him Mary was not lying and the child she was carrying was indeed from God. Verses 24 and 25 tell us he took Mary as his wife and she remained a virgin until Christ was born.

Notice Mary didn't have to do any *convincing*. There was no "But Joseph, I'm the one for you—really" coming out of Mary's mouth. Had that incident taken place today, I'm not so sure it would have turned out the same way.

My experiences from both high school and college lead me to believe that in many cases (notice I did not say all) Christian girls are usually a little more "with it" at this stage of the game and we tend to be a little more geared toward finding out God's *whole* will for our lives (including whom we will date or marry). Guys haven't usually thought this far in advance yet.

But we girls aren't always with it either. You would not believe how many girls I have met who tell me they just *know* they are "called to be a pastor's wife," and now they just need to find the pastor.

I'm not saying that God did not really reveal this as His will for those girls, but I do want to borrow a quote from Elisabeth Elliot when it comes to the guy issue (then we'll get back to Mary's story—I promise).

In her bestselling book, *Passion and Purity*, Ms. Elliot says: "Women are always tempted to be initiators. We like to get things done. We want to talk about situations and feelings, get it all out in the open, deal with it. It appears to us that men often ignore and evade issues, sweep things under the rug, forget about them, go on with projects, business, pleasures, sports, eat a big steak, turn on the television, roll over, and go to sleep. Women respond to this tendency by insisting on confrontation, communication, showdown. If we can't dragoon our men into that, we nag, we plead, we get attention by tears, silence or withholding warmth and intimacy. We have a large bag of tricks."[4]

Trusting God With Relationships

Although we can't "listen in" on Mary's conversation with Joseph, the outcome still teaches us two important things. First, it teaches we should never let our convictions and decisions be guided by our attractions—if God is calling us to do something, then we are to do it even if it costs us the affections of a guy. (It doesn't matter whether he is a godly guy or not.)

> WE SHOULD NEVER LET OUR CONVICTIONS AND DECISIONS BE GUIDED BY OUR ATTRACTIONS.

Second, we are not to try to "force" things when a certain guy does not seem to believe he fits into God's plan for our lives, no matter what we *think* God has told us. We should never use a "thus saith the Lord" in an attempt to manipulate some guy into being a part of our lives. Like Mary, we need to leave that part up to God. Let God fill the guy in on how he is (or isn't) supposed to be part of your life.

Years ago I met a guy who seemed to be a perfect fit for me. We were headed in the same direction ministry-wise—or so we thought—and it seemed to make perfect sense to seek God's will together. I began to pray, asking God if he was the one for me. I didn't know that he was also praying and asking God the very same question.

One day, much to my dismay, this guy received his answer from the Lord: I was not the one for him. At that time I didn't understand, but now, when I look and see how our lives have turned out, I see clearly that God knew what He was doing all along. Imagine what a mess I would have gotten myself into had I tried to convince him that he was part of God's will for my life.

In regard to those girls I met in college who believed they were to be pastors' wives, the problem was not in what they believed to be their call; it was in their method—thinking they could hunt down any single pastor and make him their own.

But anyway, back to Mary's story. Here she was, feeling all alone, completely shut out, and she was sitting on a donkey in a foreign town. As if that (and the initial rejection from Joseph she was probably still recovering from) was not enough, there was a whole other element to the story I had overlooked until a professor in college pointed it out to me. Joseph's whole family had to trek back to Bethlehem for the census, or at least it would appear that way since the decree recorded in Luke 2:3 stated that *everyone* must return to his own city.

The quaint little scene in the stable does not mention Mary's in-laws, so apparently they must have all had places to lay their heads. Imagine that—here Mary was, in obvious discomfort, in an unfamiliar place, going into labor with family members around, yet she is left with nowhere to go. I am just flabbergasted by that. Talk about being shut out. Her own family (or at least her in-laws) didn't even do anything to make sure her labor went smoothly or ensure that she was okay.

And to top it all off, most commentaries say the

"stable" where Mary and Joseph did end up residing was nothing more than a dark and dirty cave *used as* a stable.[5]

God, Have You Forgotten Me?

Even the manger where Jesus was placed was most likely a feeding trough just cut out of the side of the cave—think of that! Mary, Joseph, and the baby Jesus were lying on hard stone all night long. I mean, was there no relief for this poor girl who was called by God to such an awesome task?

Have you ever been camping? Not in a motor home, not on an air mattress, but full on, hard core, sleeping-under-the-stars *Survivor*-type camping? Well, if you haven't, just let me tell you that no matter how tired you are, the ground gets to be pretty uncomfortable around three or four in the morning. I imagine the feeling was ten times worse for Mary as she sat or lay on the bottom of that cave and gave birth to her firstborn son—who also happened to be the King of the world!

We have to realize that being shut out at the inn was not like accepting a simple demotion from the Hilton to Motel 6. It wasn't like spending the night at a friend's and being told you have to sleep in the garage. It was knowing you had been handpicked to do something really cool, but then finding yourself directed to the hard ground while being in excruciating pain, and sitting next to donkey droppings. I don't know for certain, but I am pretty sure Mary was caught off guard by the accommodations God arranged for her in Bethlehem.

I can imagine Mary felt pretty lonely as she and

Joseph (and perhaps a midwife who traveled with them[6]) wandered the streets looking for this cave. Can't you just hear the cries of Mary's heart that night? Think of things from her perspective for just a moment here. Can you hear her sniffles as reality sets in and she starts to cry? Poor Joseph probably just shook his head, not knowing what to do. There was no comfort he could have offered that would have been enough to calm Mary's hurting heart.

GOD, HAVE YOU FORGOTTEN ME DOWN HERE?

God, have you forgotten me down here? I can hear Mary's mind racing as her back ached, her head spun, and the labor pangs began. *I'm really scared and feel really alone, and we need a place to rest our heads. This baby You placed in me, God, the one You say is Your Son, I think He's on His way, and I don't know what to do.* I can see her drying her tears with the end of her veil and looking heavenward in despair.

Have you ever been that lonely? Has your heart ever hurt so badly you thought it would burst? I don't think I have ever been where Mary was, but I did feel pretty alone when all of my friends from church graduated before I did and moved off to college. I felt even more alone when my newfound friends took my name off the homecoming ballot and told me I didn't have what it took to be one of them.

But when I looked back in my old journal to see if I remembered that night as it really happened, I was surprised by my perspective about one thing. There was something good that I did manage to grasp in the midst of all the horror. The morning after the whole party incident, I wrote the words, "I shined my light last night," in big bold letters. And I had.

ALONE WITH GOD

Mary shined her light that night in Bethlehem too. I know at that point it was too late for Mary to back out of birthing the Savior of the world, but she did not have to be as obedient as she was in the months and years that followed. The Bible does not give us details regarding what went down in that cave, but I can imagine all of Mary's loneliness faded away the second she heard the first cry of the baby Jesus.

Holding Him in her arms was probably all it took to make Mary forget about how hard the ground was. In that moment, she was probably thankful for the privacy of the cave—she didn't have to share the experience of what it felt like to hold God himself in her arms. In perhaps one of the loneliest moments in Mary's life up until that point, God showed up, and nothing has been the same for any of us since.

God has a tendency to do that. He shows up when we are shut out. And usually it is only then that we can see our "shutting out" was divinely orchestrated. I remember one particular evening during my sophomore year of college when I reached a breaking point. It had been a rough week. I didn't like my job, I had just finished some big tests and projects, and I had some looming decisions to make—in particular, one about whether or not I was going to lead a missions trip.

It was a Wednesday night. My evening class was cancelled, and none of my friends were around. I called home to talk with my parents, and there was no answer there either. So I grabbed my Bible, got in my car, and drove to the midweek Bible study at church. It was uncharacteristic of me to go alone because I was still fairly new to the area and I did not know anyone at the church aside from my friends from school who went with me.

I carefully selected a seat somewhere in the center of the sanctuary and kept glancing at the back door as people filed in, as if I were expecting somebody. I did this to discourage any of the greeters from coming over and chatting with me. Like I said, it had been a long week and I didn't feel like talking. That night there was a guest speaker—someone I had heard many times before at youth camp.

"GOD WORKS HARD TO GET US ALONE."

The irony of his words made me stifle a giggle as I sat there, an island in a sea of people. He said, "God works hard to get us alone." He went on to talk about how each of the people in the Bible whom God called to do great things had to initially endure a time of seeming loneliness or feeling "shut out."

He talked about a few other things that night, and I couldn't take notes fast enough. There in that sanctuary, all alone and completely worn out, God confirmed to me I was in fact supposed to lead that missions trip—and that trip became an event in my life that dramatically shaped my character and changed who I was.

Perhaps God had to get Mary alone so she could feel the drastic difference in her circumstances after Jesus was born; she never had to be alone again. Maybe I had to go through the stinging pain of standing up for my convictions at the beginning of my senior year in high school so that at the end of the school year, when I stood up as one of the top candidates for prom queen, I would know I was there *because* of my convictions, not *in spite* of them.

And I honestly believe God had to get me alone that night in college in order to confirm to me that I was in fact supposed to lead that trip. God often comes in unconventional ways, and for some reason He tends to take great pleasure in coming to us when we are alone.

If you are reading this and you feel even in the slightest way as if you are being shut out—then take joy, my friend—a major blessing is on its way. This loneliness is just your training ground for greatness. It is simply God's way of singling you out for whatever it is He has in store for you.

One of my favorite devotionals, *Streams in the Desert,* contains the following quote: "God is continually preparing His heroes, and when the opportunity is right, He puts them into position in an instant. He works so fast, the world wonders where they came from."[7]

The world wonders where God's heroes come from because they are often those who are lonely, forgotten, isolated, or shut out. Sometimes they come from caves, like Mary did—and the hard circumstances and dim lighting were just what they needed to prepare them for the exclusive tasks God has for them.

There's no telling where all of "God's heroes" will come from, and there is no telling just how shut out they will have to feel before God comes on the scene. If your heart is hurting as you read these words, be encouraged. God is on His way. Dry your eyes, lift your head, and listen for the cry of a baby in Bethlehem who came to this world through a scared and lonely girl sitting on a hard cave floor.

That same King—the One who came in an unlikely situation to a girl who was feeling more than just a little shut out—is the very One who is in control of your life, and He has an awesome plan for you.

Look around your cave. Is the floor hard? Is the lighting bad? Is your family nowhere to be found? Do your friends all seem far away?

Mary's been there too—and look what God did with her life. So settle in and get comfortable. Start expecting a miracle, and before you know it you'll also forget how hard the ground is as you enjoy the presence of God.

6

KEEPSAKES AND TREASURES

"Mary treasured all these things,
pondering them in her heart."
—Luke 2:19

While rummaging around in the garage, I was dripping with sweat from moving so many heavy boxes on a hot summer's day. Blowing at a stray strand of hair that fell in my face, I rested my hands on my hips and surveyed the display of half-opened boxes before me. "My old journals have to be here somewhere," I muttered to myself as I threw back the lid of another cardboard treasure chest.

I stopped cold. There, sitting in the box—nestled between some of my favorite books I thought I had loaned out and lost—was my old Bible. It was the Bible I had used when I first became serious about God, at the end of junior high and into early high school.

Gingerly I lifted it from the darkness and held it close to my chest. It was an old *Teen Study Bible* with a bright pink cover. Just one look at it reminded me of all the journeys that particular book and I had traveled together.

It went with me to summer camp and winter camp several times (dried flowers from those getaways were still pressed between the pages); that Bible even traveled with me to Europe on my first missions trip when I was barely fifteen.

I immediately halted the search for my misplaced journals—I had found something more important. Who needed to read *my* words when I had *God's* Word right in front of me? When I opened the fragile pages of the dusty old Bible, my face broke into a smile. There, on page after page of God's promises, was a massive amount of highlighting and underlining, as well as many notes scrawled in my youthful handwriting in the margins.

Next to some verses I had even written dates and a word or two to remind me of what God had said to me personally. There was such freshness exemplified in those pages—everything was new to me back then. I became a Christian at the age of four, but there was something about my passion for God at the age of fourteen and fifteen that now made me jealous for that kind of fervor again.

On those pages was evidence that when I initially fell in love with God I fell hard. I treasured His Word to me as if it were a collection of love letters, and if I closed my eyes I could still quote some passages from memory. After spending a good portion of time leafing through the pages of my old Bible, I turned and picked up my "new" Bible, the one I had been using for the past several years.

It was a different translation, with smaller print and

a leather cover, but there was highlighting and margin scrawlings in it also. In that moment I suddenly thought of Mary—and how she had treasured the things God told her and "pondered them in her heart." *The Message* translation says Mary held all of those things "dear, deep within herself."

There are two specific times when the Bible says Mary treasured the things God told her. The first was in Luke 2:19, on the night Christ was born and the shepherds came to visit. The second was in Luke 2:51, when Jesus was a young boy—probably about twelve years old—and He got separated from His parents on their family trip to the Feast of Passover because He was with the temple scholars, astonishing them with His wisdom regarding spiritual things.

I'm sure there were many more moments in Mary's life when she treasured God's words to her. She was just a girl when her journey with God began, and she was still a fairly young woman when Jesus left her to return to heaven. In the days and years following His ascension, I'm sure that Mary pulled out bucket loads of memories and basked in the warmth spilling from them. She probably enjoyed recounting her life with Jesus to the disciples and the early church. And on the days Mary missed Him— missed His smile, His touch, and the sound of His voice—her memories of life with Jesus probably brought great comfort.

Mary mastered the art of pondering what God told her—*before* she understood it. Only later, as time unfolded God's reasoning and explained some of His plans, was she truly able to treasure just what each thing meant to her.

MARY MASTERED THE ART OF PONDERING WHAT GOD TOLD HER— BEFORE SHE UNDERSTOOD IT.

In my imagination I see a middle-aged version of Mary, leaning against the windowsill and looking out at children playing in the street. Tears wet her eyes, and she wipes at them with the bottom corner of her headpiece. *Jesus was such a perfect little boy,* she thinks as a curly-haired four-year-old runs to catch up with his siblings.

Her mind takes her back to a time when life was different—to a time when the whole world was different. *Jesus was always so good to His brothers and sisters. He was always so good to the whole world.* A sob chokes her as she thinks of the wretched day at Calvary and the events leading up to the crucifixion of her son, but joy conquers the grief as she remembers the empty tomb.

She could close her eyes and almost hear the sound of His cry on the night He was born; in an instant her mind could flash forward to the cry He made from the cross at Calvary. A sword must have pierced her heart, the place where Mary kept her memories, every time *that* memory surfaced. It was the one that brought her the most grief, but closer examination shows it is also the one that brought her the most joy.

Because of that bone-chilling afternoon at the cross, Mary was promised eternity with her son. Not only that—because of that afternoon, Jesus became more than just Mary's son. He was her Savior as well. By taking Him at His word and keeping the secrets He shared with her hidden in her heart, Mary was no longer just the mother of Jesus—she was His disciple too. She became a student of her Lord, and we should be His students as well. We must pay careful attention to the things He shows us and to the things He shares with us through His Word.

CHARTING OUR JOURNEY

It is important to chart our journeys with God. As an old friend used to say, we should "litter our lives with altars." She meant that we should set up reminders for ourselves of what God has done for us in the past. Thinking back to earlier times has often encouraged me. I have traveled back through the pages of my journals many times, both to dark nights and new dawns. I have often seen the hand of God in hindsight where I hadn't seen Him before by tracing back through situations recorded in my own handwriting.

If you do not keep a journal (or diary) already, then I strongly suggest you start. Record everything—your thoughts, your goals, your experiences, events, verses that are speaking to you at the moment, and even your prayers. Keep your journal somewhere safe, and every now and then take a journey through your past. Chances are you will be amazed to see just how faithful and gracious God was to you. Have you ever noticed the words *journey* and *journal* are similar? Hmm . . . I wonder why that is.

I love reading entries from when I first began walking

with God. I was so excited I could barely put my thoughts into words. Every now and then I pull one of my old journals off the shelf to see where I was a year or two earlier. I remember a recent moment when an old journal entry really shocked me; on those pages was clear evidence that God was working behind the scenes in my life long before I ever realized it.

In June 2002 I began to pursue a lifelong dream by writing my first book. At that time, as I sat and apprehensively tapped out page after page, I had no clue the book would even be published. One month into the adventure, I sat down to reflect on an author who contributed greatly to my own spiritual growth as a teen. In my journal I wrote these words:

> *What I admire most about Robin Jones Gunn is her legacy, and I hope to one day touch lives with my writing the way she has touched mine. . . . I hope I can one day carry her torch.*

Two days short of being exactly one year later, I sat at breakfast with Robin—I was a published author and she wrote the foreword for my first book! The ironic part is that I forgot about the journal entry (although I never forgot about her impact on me) and I had nothing to do with her writing the foreword. God divinely arranged it in His own way. Since then Robin and I have become good friends.

I'm glad I charted that moment in my life. When I found the journal entry I was taken aback—the reflection on the past made me praise God all the more in the present for the awesome thing He was doing.

There are other entries through the years that make me cringe at my own immaturity and laugh at my own ignorance. I wrote about petty fights with friends, the fear of leaving for college, and the dilemma over whether or not to change my major (which I did three times).

We tend to forget the details as we go along in our lives. God doesn't, of course. He knows why things play out exactly as they do. Keeping a journal is a way of learning the "missed lessons" of the past. It is a way to tangibly see how you have grown and changed, and to measure what really went on "behind the scenes" in the story

> MANY TIMES THE REAL STORY OF OUR LIVES CAN BE READ BETWEEN THE LINES.

of your life. Journals are also great ways to look back and see how God spent months and years preparing you for certain things. Many times the real story of our lives can be read between the lines.

WHEN GOD SPEAKS

A significant verse that is underlined in my Bible is Psalm 30:5: "Weeping may endure for a night, but joy comes in the morning" (NKJV). Next to it, in blue ink, is a date—it was the night I fully surrendered my life to Christ. I was sitting alone in my room, bawling my eyes out, when God brought the verse to my attention.

The scrawling in the margin tells the story of how God met me where I was and taught me to walk with Him. Now I have many treasured verses with dates next to them, each telling a different story of God's faithfulness to me. It's important for us to highlight the verses God uses to take us down His paths for us.

Along with reading through my own journal, I sometimes read the journals of other Christians because they can really speak to me. One told a particularly moving story. After his death, the wife of martyred missionary Jim Elliot published his journals. In the last sentence, in the last entry before Jim went out to meet his death, are the words "Let spirit conquer though the flesh conspire."[1] The Spirit did conquer through Jim's life, because those who conspired against him and killed him were eventually brought to Christ. His words were poignantly prophetic, even though he probably did not know it at the time.

Todd Beamer, hero of United flight 93 on September 11, 2001, kept a stack of Scripture cards in his car. Each day he would recite a verse and memorize it as he drove. In her touching book, *Let's Roll*, his widow, Lisa, tells how the card on top of his stack on September 11 brought great comfort to her hurting heart.

Romans 11:33–36 first hit home with Lisa earlier in her life, when her father passed away. The passage stood as a mile marker for her on her spiritual journey. And on September 11 it is believed that is the last passage of Scripture Todd Beamer ever read. It says:

Oh, the depth of the riches of the wisdom and knowledge of God! How unsearchable his judgments, and his paths beyond tracing out! "Who has known the mind of the Lord? Or who has been his counselor?"

"Who has ever given to God, that God should repay him?" For from him and through him and to him are all things. To him be the glory forever! Amen. (NIV)

In her own words, Lisa describes what finding that card meant to her:

It was the exact passage of Scripture that had helped me through my questions following my dad's death; the same passage I had been reminded of at Wheaton College; and the very passage that had been my memory verse for the Bible study I was preparing in Rome, the week before Todd died. Seeing the card reminded me that God is always speaking to us and giving us just the words we need for the events he knows lie ahead.[2]

Stones of Remembrance

Like Mary, we all need to remember the things God has shown us. Like Joshua and the Israelites, we need to pick up stones of remembrance upon our path because God is constantly offering promises for us to stand on and hidden gems of His wisdom to cling to as we travel through our daily lives.

In Joshua 4, God commands the children of Israel to pick up twelve stones from the Jordan River as a reminder of the time the waters were cut off at the feet of the priests and the Ark of the Covenant was brought over. Verse seven tells the reason behind the command: "So these stones shall become a memorial to the sons of Israel forever." Future generations would be able to look back and attest to God's faithfulness to their ancestors because stones of remembrance were established.

For a while, after reading that passage for the first time, I collected real stones from places I went—prayer walks with God, missions trips, and youth camps—and on the bottom I would write in permanent marker the date and a verse or a word to remind myself of what God was teaching me. I kept my treasures on a shelf in my room as a tangible reminder of where I had been, where I was going, and what God was teaching me. Eventually my collection grew too large to maintain, and I decided my journal was a good enough reminder of what God was showing me.

What has God done for you in your life? And what do you have that stands as a testimony? If you were to die today, could someone else trace your spiritual journey and be encouraged? Yes, Mary pondered the things God had told her and she openly spoke about those things so that they might be preserved. In fact, the story of Christ's birth recounted in Luke is believed to be there only because she sat down with Luke and told him her story as he was writing his gospel.[3] Mary left a legacy—and a paper trail—of all God did for her. She wanted others to know of God's faithfulness to her, and you should too.

Along with keeping a journal, I would encourage you to read the journal of someone else—and I don't mean sneaking a peek at your best friend's diary when she isn't looking! Spiritual biographies or journals of those who have gone before us in the faith are something that can really encourage us because they offer vulnerable glimpses into other people's hearts and thoughts. Sometimes look-ing at their struggles and victories can be like a mirror. Many times we see ourselves in the reflection of others.

In college, after I led a missions trip through the Stu-dent Missionary Union (SMU) on campus, they asked all of us leaders to write our thoughts on what it was like to lead a trip. It was a means of sharing some of the lessons God had taught us along the way. The staff at SMU was going to take our musings and compile a journal to give to new leaders in coming years, to encourage and inspire them as they planned and led their own trips.

Up Close and Personal

It is vital to your spiritual health that you make your rela-tionship with Christ personal—it is about you and God, and how you relate to and communicate with Him. If your heart is not full of things to ponder, and you haven't taken up any stones of remembrance, then you are missing out on the depth of relationship God desires to have with you!

Being girls, I know we tend to become very nostalgic when it comes to certain things. When a hot guy gives us a flower, what do we do with it? We usually dry it out and save it. When we go to the movies with our friends—or on a first date—what do we do with the stub? We keep it and put

> IT IS VITAL TO YOUR SPIRITUAL HEALTH THAT YOU MAKE YOUR RELATIONSHIP WITH CHRIST PERSONAL.

it in a scrapbook or some other safe place. We need to treat the special keepsakes and treasures God gives us in the same manner and with the same amount of care— even if at times they are less tangible than movie stubs and dried flowers.

We need to interact with God's Word in such a way that we allow God to speak to specific situations in our lives. A good way to develop a habit of being in God's Word—and being able to hear what He is saying to you—is to get a daily devotional to help guide you through the pages of Scripture. One of my favorites is the classic, *Streams in the Desert*. Or maybe you can start with one of those "read the Bible in one year" plans.

Keeping a record of things we ask God for in prayer and how He answers us is a good way to be aware of just how intricately God works in our lives, whether it is with the answer we were looking for or not. A friend of mine spent years praying for her future husband. She spent a lot of time writing out her prayers for this man and writing out what she believed God was showing her about him at the time.

At one point as she was praying and journaling, she believed God was showing her he was not in the United States. Over time, she got tired of waiting and exclaimed, "God is just going to have to bring this guy to me in the supermarket one day because I don't know where I am going to find him!"

Years later, when God's timing was right, God brought her husband to her—in the local neighborhood Costco! As she got to know him, she was amazed at how accurate the things she documented in her journal were. He was even out of the country doing missions work at the time she wrote about God showing her that in her journal. Her journal was full of prayers God answered in specific detail; it was a great way to look back and praise God for what He had done.

Think about the things you treasure. Are the promises of God among the things you hold dearest? If your house burned to the ground tonight, taking all of your tangible possessions with it, would the core of your life still be intact or would it all turn to ash and dust with your belongings?

There is a quote written in the margin of my old Bible I found in the garage, and I was surprised to see it there since it is written in the margin of my new Bible too. In thick bold letters I wrote, "Remember in the dark what God has shown you in the light." That is what it means to treasure the things God told you and keep them in your heart. It means no matter what—just like Mary— you can see God is telling you the exact words you need to hear for whatever comes next. It means you have learned from the journey you have been on thus far, and your ears and heart are tuned to hear what God is going to say next.

In the Old Testament, God used to instruct the prophets to write down the things He was showing them. Habakkuk 2:2 says, "Then the Lord answered me and said, 'Record the vision and inscribe it on tablets that the one who reads it may run.'"

What about your life? Are you inscribing the things

God has shown you? Are you "pondering" things in your heart like Mary did? Is the way you have been marking your journey enough to send someone running toward Jesus right now?

God's words might not always be understandable right away. But write them down and reflect on them. Give God a little time to explain what's going on. I'm sure Mary didn't really understand why the shepherds were flocking to her Son and kneeling before Him on the night of His birth; she probably didn't even understand how they *found* Him.

But Mary loved God and she loved to hear from God. And that is the only example we need. If you found yourself hungry to hear from God as you read this chapter, then I suggest you pick up your Bible and put this book down. It's time to grab a pad of paper, a highlighter, and a pen as you set out to find some stones of remembrance you alone can treasure.

7

ALWAYS AMAZED

"And His father and mother were amazed at
the things which were being said about Him."
—Luke 2:33

My friend Zach is one of my favorite people ever. I think he is just an absolutely awesome kid, and I love him like a little brother. It has been a privilege to watch him grow from a pudgy-fisted little boy into a godly young man.

One afternoon, just before spring break during Zach's senior year of high school, the local Chevy dealer drove onto his high school campus in a new truck and handed him the keys and a stack of hundred-dollar bills—a gift from an anonymous person who thought Zach was a great guy who deserved a special blessing. Jotted on a note, his only instructions were:

> *... The money is for your summer. You're only eighteen once*
> *and you only have one senior summer, so enjoy it. God has a great*
> *adventure in store for you. Love Him with all your heart....*

Everyone in the parking lot was stunned. There was

no logical explanation for what had occurred. People don't normally send paid-for trucks and stacks of cash to high school kids on random Wednesday afternoons—although many of us probably wish they would.

Amazed would be a good word to describe Zach's response that day. This was definitely a blessing he had not seen coming that morning when he rolled out of bed to go to school. I'm sure it wasn't the first thing that came to his mind when he was called out of class and into the office either.

A few days before this blessing arrived, Zach was in a minor car accident and was going to have to have his old van—affectionately known as "Lawanda"—repaired. And just the day before his new truck arrived, Zach's sister Mical got her driver's license—yet had nothing to drive.

So not only was this a blessing for Zach, it was a blessing for Mical too. How perfect was that? God is awesome. He always rewards those who diligently seek Him, and for years I have watched Zach diligently seek Him. Many times the abundance of God's blessings leaves us speechless and amazed.

Mary knew her son wasn't an average boy; she was well aware from the very beginning that Jesus was the Son of God. Yet, she was still amazed at the things she saw when she watched His life on earth unfold. Although God had told her about this miracle that would take place in her life before it actually occurred, Mary still had moments when she was stunned speechless by what was going on.

Do you ever have moments like that? You know the

ones I'm talking about—where you sit there thinking, *No way. This is such a God thing. It's so, so, so impossible.* Impossible. What a great word. God must love it when we use it because it opens the floodgates for Him to move the things in our lives, changing the ordinary to the extraordinary in a matter of minutes.

Yesterday when I flipped my daily Scripture calendar, I found these words beneath the verse of the day: "Difficulty is the very atmosphere of miracle—it is a miracle in its first stage. If it is to be a great miracle, the condition is not difficulty but impossibility."[1]

We all wake up to impossible or difficult things at one point or another, and some days we wake up to things that are really quite miraculous. But when we find ourselves enrolled in God's school of faith, we are often surprised to find that the word *impossible* does not appear on God's vocabulary list.

THE WORD *IMPOSSIBLE* DOES NOT APPEAR ON GOD'S VOCABULARY LIST.

As we now know, Mary's life went from the mundane to the miraculous in a matter of minutes. She had God's favor, and He ruled her heart. So, when He saw fit, He rearranged her life with one quick turn of His hand. Sometimes He does the same with us. In an instant He pulls back the veil and shows us His face, or with a snap of His fingers a wall crumbles and we are led forth into new places.

Other times, God moves slowly and we can only see

glimpses of His glory peeking through the cracks in His fingers as He holds our lives in His hands. In Psalm 31:15 David acknowledges that his times are in God's hands. Jesus reminds us in Acts 1:7 that it is not up to us to know the times or seasons; the timing of the events of our lives is up to God alone. We are not to try to rush ahead of Him or force His hand.

Many times the things He will do—and the timing of those things—will leave us amazed at the attention God puts into the little details. In retrospect, we can usually see the pieces of our lives fitting together like a puzzle, creating a picture we could never imagine in the beginning.

SHOCK AND WONDER

I remember September 11, 2001, very well. I was in college and was awakened by panicked phone calls from my mom and my roommate's mom as they tearfully informed us that our nation was under attack. My dorm-mates and I spent the day planted in front of the television and attending an emergency chapel service to pray for our country.

A few months later I walked into the Student Missionary Union office on campus—where I was working as a secretary at the time—and went straight to the president's office. We were friends, so I felt comfortable sharing my heart with him.

"Look," I said, trying to hide my frustration, "I understand why we are sending teams all over the world. The world needs Jesus. But I think it's terrible that our own country needs Him right now and we are doing nothing about it."

He looked at me with a smirk before answering. "I was hoping you would come to me," he said. "I think you should lead a trip." I was stunned. I was already on a team being sent from my church to "ground zero" that December. How was I going to be able to lead another team back there over spring break? I couldn't raise funds like that—I just couldn't do two missions trips in six months. Or so I thought. My reason for coming to him was to find *someone else* to lead a trip.

When a few minutes lapsed and I still hadn't answered, my friend finally said, "Pray about it and get back to me. But [the staff] talked about it last week and we think you should lead the trip." In the days and weeks that followed, the details came together to confirm to me that God had in fact called me to lead this trip. And when applications went out to the student body, we had more applicants for that trip than many of the other trips combined. Our university went and made a lasting impact at ground zero, all because with a quick turn of His hand God put me in the right place at the right time and gave me the strength to lead.

At first, I was amazed simply by getting the call. But the true wonder came when my team and I were in New York watching God use us to change the lives of men and women touched by tragedy. I was even more stunned, though, by what happened later.

About a year and a half after my trip, I was doing a radio interview for a Christian talk show in Chicago. It lasted about half an hour, and I remember hanging up the phone wondering if anyone had even heard the interview or knew about my new book that was just published.

A few months later I received a letter from the radio station, telling me about a man who called in after the show saying he had met me at ground zero and I had made a lasting impact on his life. He called the station to find out where he could go and buy my book. The letter moved me to tears because this man was not a Christian, but he was still desperately searching for God.

He was someone I remembered praying for and witnessing to but just couldn't seem to get through to—or so I thought. *I hadn't seen this coming.* There was no previous indication that I had impacted that man's spiritual life. Without my knowing it, God was still using me at ground zero long after the cleanup process was over.

I think it delights God when we are amazed about stuff like that. As He watches His plan for our lives unfold from heaven, it probably makes Him smile when our hearts are filled with wonder and our eyes marvel at what we see. Many times He must laugh to himself as He reaches over and gently picks our open jaws up off the ground.

FINDING WAYS TO SURPRISE US

On the day Mary and Joseph took the baby Jesus to be dedicated in the temple they were met by Simeon the prophet, who had waited his whole life to see the Christ. Mary and Joseph were truly amazed at the things Simeon was saying about their son. As they began to see Jesus fulfilling age-old prophecies, the magnitude of who He really was must have begun to sink in.

God was probably sitting in heaven smiling as He thought, *I told you this child was special, Mary; I told you He was going to be the Son of God. If you think this is amazing, just wait until you see what is going to happen next.*

Being all-knowing, God can never be surprised. So He must really enjoy being able to give surprises. One year, while in high school, my friends and I planned a pretty elaborate surprise party for our friend Ruby. We came up with clues that would lead her on an adventure all over town, and with each clue she would pick up one of her friends. The final clue would lead to the rest of her friends waiting at her favorite restaurant.

> HE IS CONSTANTLY FINDING WAYS TO SURPRISE US WITH HIS GOODNESS AND AMAZE US WITH HIS LOVE.

We kidnapped her and executed our plan perfectly, strictly adhering to our previously arranged schedule. The look on her face in the end was worth it—she thought the adventure hunt was celebration enough, and we surprised her even more with the party.

We worked behind the scenes for days, making plans. We orchestrated things carefully, arranging for people to be at the right place at the right time. It was so much fun for all of us—especially because we knew how much she was going to love the party in the end.

That is how God works in our lives. He is constantly

finding ways to surprise us with His goodness and amaze us with His love. As if the cross of Calvary wasn't enough, God still generously bestows gracious and undeserved blessings upon His children.

Sometimes God really catches us off guard when we witness drastic changes in the lives of other people. I went to a large public high school, and throughout my years there, I watched some of my classmates make some bad choices, with pretty devastating consequences. One girl I knew lived life as if it were a party, and when she went off to college, her high school lifestyle carried over. In a matter of months she found herself pregnant and was forced to drop out of school.

I remember hearing about it from another friend when I was home for a weekend. I said a quick prayer for this girl whenever she crossed my mind, but I thought a turnaround in her life would be nothing short of miraculous.

Recently I was amazed to receive an e-mail from this girl, telling me she had accepted Christ three years ago, just before her son was born, and she has been walking with the Lord ever since. We were never close, but she came across a flyer for an event I was speaking at and got my e-mail address off my Web site.

She said she had to let me know what the Lord had done in her life. She didn't know I had prayed for her. The transformation in this girl was so radical that I sat at my computer with tears in my eyes as I read her e-mail—I wanted to call everyone I knew and tell them about what God did!

No one is beyond redemption's reach. That's why it is vitally important that we pray for all the unsaved people the Lord has brought into our lives. We may not always get to see the results of our prayers, but we have to trust that God is at work in the lives of those we are praying for in ways we cannot see. It is in situations like these that we should *expect* to be amazed at what God does— even if He doesn't do it in our timing.

Years ago, when my friends Desi and Rose were engaged, they told me about a somewhat bizarre discovery they made over the previous weekend. While sifting through Desi's childhood photos at his parents' house, they came across one of those large souvenir photos from a summer camp Desi attended.

Upon closer examination, Rose realized it was the same camp she grew up going to ... and she was in the same photo! They had spent a whole week at the same camp one summer and never crossed paths (or at least not in a memorable way). Yet years later, in Bible college, God brought them together, and they have now been married for years and have three of the cutest kids on the planet.

Isn't that amazing? God knows just the right moment to make our paths intersect with other people—whether it is an old friend, a stranger who needs Christ, or our future spouses. There are no coincidences in God's kingdom.

THERE ARE NO COINCIDENCES IN GOD'S KINGDOM.

Another friend received a full-ride scholarship to a

local university, but she decided to leave the state and pursue other things. Years later, when she met the man she would marry, they discovered that he had attended that university at the same time she would have been enrolled. Because it was a small school, their paths would have crossed in college, but God led her down a different path. In spite of that, she *still* ended up with the person God had for her all along. That's pretty amazing.

Sometimes amazement comes from the exciting reality that God is leading us out into new places. Other times it comes from the sparkling realization that the things we have desperately been searching for have been in front of us all along. Amazement comes anytime God catches us off guard and exceeds our expectations.

HANDLING THE CRITICS AND SKEPTICS

Mary must have lived her life in that frame of mind. Just think about some of the things she witnessed— watching Jesus turning water to wine, hearing about how her son fed the multitudes with five barley loaves and two measly fish, having people inform her when Jesus healed the sick and raised the dead.

These are not normal things. This wasn't like having the next-door neighbor say, "Hey, Mary, I heard Jesus made the honor roll. Way to go!" No, it was like having the whole neighborhood saying, "Have you heard what your son is doing? He is performing miracles. He says He is the Son of God!"

Imagine how difficult it would have been if Mary's amazement was met with the neighbors' skepticism. Mary was *amazed* because she *believed*. But what about those who didn't? How was she supposed to respond to them?

In all of our lives I'm sure we can pinpoint a few critics and skeptics—you know exactly who I am talking about. These people seem to find a negative way to look at absolutely everything. So what do we say to them when they meet us in our amazement and try to talk us out of the sense of wonder we are caught up in?

I'm learning that amazement is all a matter of perspective. I recently received an e-mail from a girl who attended a conference I had spoken at just a few days before.

"God is blessing my life and causing me to grow," she said. "We can all gain new knowledge of Him every day. Isn't it so awesome how mysterious God is? I love it. It gives me a yearning for Him and more of a passion for His Word."

This girl wakes up with a new sense of wonder and amazement *every day*. She is in awe not only of what God is doing but also of who God is. We should all strive to be more like her. The same God who created you created everything. If that reality is not enough to take our breath away, then something is wrong with our perspective.

In the midst of all our wonder at the things God is doing—and has done—we must never lose our sense of amazement at who God is. Perhaps He sometimes pulls back from doing the miraculous in our lives to remind us that we aren't ever to marvel at the miracle but at the Miracle Worker.

We should meditate on verses like Exodus 15:11,

which says, "Who is like You, majestic in holiness, awesome in praises, working wonders?" Psalm 77:14 echoes that verse by saying, "You are the God who works wonders." And Psalm 18:30 (NIV) wraps it all up beautifully by saying, "As for God, his way is perfect."

THERE IS MORE TO LIFE THAN JUST WHAT I CAN SEE.

With verses like that to lean on, how can we *not* be amazed? Some mornings I wake up and am instantly overcome by the reality that there is more to life than just what I can see. God is working behind the scenes to make sure everything in the entire universe is working as it should be. He is bringing answers to prayers I have been praying for, sometimes for quite some time, though I cannot see them yet.

Each morning all of us should wake up well aware of the fact that there is more to our lives than meets the eye. God is at work up in heaven, turning the times and the seasons and prompting the hearts of other people in ways that will ultimately affect us.

So when skeptics come to us and try to tell us that our God is just too big to be real, we need to tell them (kindly), "The problem isn't God." The problem is that too many people have eyes that are far too small. Because they cannot see the whole picture, they cannot see what is really going on.

Late Christian recording artist Rich Mullins once said, "There are places to go that cannot be seen, and the scope of our vision is too small for our strides. Faith is not a denial of facts—it is a broadening of focus."[2]

Living in amazement requires a broadening of focus—it requires catching a vision much larger than yourself. The skeptics who most likely came to Mary, and the ones who will most certainly come to you, don't have any vision—or at least not any vision based on truth. And Proverbs 29:18 says, "Where there is no vision, the people perish" (KJV).

The sense of vision I am talking about here is not a belief in some weird urban legend or grasping for a mirage in the desert. Vision isn't hallucinating or seeing only what we want to see. It's looking past what we can see to what has been there all along. It's waking up every morning and being infused with the very breath of God. As children of God, we are called to bask in the reality that we are only a small part of a much greater story. Having vision simply means seeing God in everything.

We need to face each day with a sense of wonder and amazement. There is nothing our God cannot do. Mary saw it in her lifetime, and if we live with an attitude of expectancy, we will too. When the time is right, God will enter our circumstances, changing them drastically with a slight turn of His hand. Then the skeptics and the faithful will be amazed together.

8

WORRIED AND CONFUSED

*"But they [Mary and Joseph] did not
understand the statement which He
[Jesus] had made to them."*
—Luke 2:50

Her face lit up as she recounted her day to me. "I was at the beach early this morning in my usual spot," my mom—an avid sailor—said. "I sat there just watching the horizon, letting the cool breeze brush across my face. In the distance I watched the fog roll across the water. I began to pray and thank God for His beautiful creation, and before I knew it the fog had crept up and engulfed me. I couldn't see the water or the sand. I couldn't see a foot in front of me."

She smiled and paused for emphasis before making her point. "Sometimes the spiritual life is like that," she said, looking into the distance, her voice trailing off. "The fog rolls in and you can't see a thing even though things were perfectly clear only moments before."

I nodded slowly as she spoke. The picture she was painting was so clear, so perfect to describe Mary's story—

ıd perhaps yours as well. When Jesus was twelve years old, His family made their annual trek to the temple. But on this particular pilgrimage Jesus stayed behind (without their knowledge) when everyone else packed up and returned to Nazareth.

One day into their journey home, Mary and Joseph realized Jesus was not mixed in among the other children and family members, and they panicked. After three days of frantic searching, they found Him—sitting in the midst of the rabbis, amazing them with His extensive knowledge and understanding of the Scriptures.

Mary's first words to Him, recorded in Luke 2:48, were, "Son, why have You treated us this way? Behold, Your father and I have been anxiously looking for You." And as if the whole missing-child thing were not enough to worry the poor girl, Jesus' answer probably left her a little more than confused. In verse 49 He said, "Why is it that you were looking for Me? Did you not know that I had to be in My Father's house?"

Can't you just see Mary's tearstained face, weary with worry, her brow scrunched in bewilderment? What did Jesus mean by *that*? I can see her with dark circles under her eyes from the sleep she missed while worrying about where Jesus was. She blinks at Him in confusion, looking to Joseph, who can only answer her with a shrug.

Who are You? Mary probably had many moments when she didn't understand—or even recognize—Jesus as He grew up and began to embrace His role as Savior of the world. That day as He sat in the synagogue amazing the scholars, I can see Mary shaking her head and wondering,

Is this the same kid whose tears I wiped away when He fell and skinned His knee?

Have you ever felt like that? Has the fog rolled into your life lately? Are you looking at your circumstances and casting a glance heavenward, asking, *God, where are You?*

Many times I have been thoroughly convinced I was on the right path, only to have the fog roll in and either slow me down or turn me around completely. I know the Bible clearly states that God is with us in the storms of life, when we are getting tossed around and beaten up. But what about in the fog? What about when we cannot even see where to step in order to move? Is God still there when the way before us clouds over, plans change, and our dreams come to nothing?

God usually allows the fog to roll into our lives to remind us that His plan is different than our own. Isaiah 45:2 says, "I will go before you and make the rough places smooth." Jeremiah 29:11 says, " 'For I know the plans that I have for you,' declares the LORD, 'plans for welfare and not for calamity to give you a future and a hope.' "

GOD'S DREAMS

I was at a retreat recently where the speaker said she once asked the Lord, "Do you have dreams, God? Do you have dreams for your children?" She went on to talk about how our own dreams often get in the way of the bigger dreams God has for us. God has huge dreams for His children—dreams far bigger than we can even fathom. We aren't always able to see that, though.

OUR OWN DREAMS OFTEN GET IN THE WAY OF THE BIGGER DREAMS GOD HAS FOR US.

Along with Mary, another great woman of God who knew what it felt like to have the fog set in was Gladys Aylward. Earlier in her life, Gladys had read a magazine article about China that tugged at her heart. She was certain she heard God's call. So in her twenties she attempted to answer the call and enrolled in the Women's Training Center at the China Inland Mission—only to be told she scored too low on the theology assignments and was not up to par with other students.

Defeated and nearly drowning in fog, she returned to her parents' house confused, disappointed, and unsure of what to do next. Worrying about how she was going to make ends meet, Gladys returned to her former profession as a housekeeper. But as she did so, she heard the call growing louder, not fainter. Her heart still burned with passion for China. Repeatedly she asked God what He was doing; she did not understand why the call would come only to have the way blocked.

God answered *a few years later* when, through channels she did not plan to pass through, Gladys made it to China just in time to take over the ministry of the ailing and elderly Jeannie Lawson.[1] Note: It took Gladys *years* to move through her fog.

Other biblical illustrations of how God used the fog to delay a journey are found in the lives of the apostle

Paul, Jacob's son Joseph, Ruth the Moabite, and King David. Look at how long Paul wanted to go to Rome. Romans 15:22 tells us he made many attempts to get there but was stopped along the way because God had other places for Him to minister in first.

If Paul would have made it to Rome when he first wanted to go, our Bibles would only have sixty-five books in them because he would not have written Romans. There would have been no need for that letter had Paul been able to get there right away, and Christians today would be poorer for not having the teaching of that great book of the Bible.

Don't you think Paul must have been confused when God kept shutting the door to Rome? His heart was good, he desired to serve God there ... so why was the way blocked? I would guess that Paul experienced some confusion over that matter.

Joseph would probably have spent the rest of his life serving in Potiphar's house (instead of being exalted to the number-two spot in all of Egypt and saving the world from famine) had God not allowed him to be hauled off to prison on false charges and put in a foggy and confusing holding cell as Genesis 39–45 explains. I am sure there were more than a few moments when he feared for his life!

Ruth would never have met and married Boaz (and produced Obed, who was in the line of Jesus) had she not first married Naomi's son, Chilion, who later died. As a soon-to-be bride, I cannot imagine Ruth's grief as a young widow. In many ways she probably thought her life was over and could never have imagined the joy yet to come. If she had never been a widow, she would have never known Naomi, left Moab, or met Boaz. And most importantly, Ruth would not have come to know the true and living God.

David—the very man after God's own heart—was not ready to be king on the day Samuel anointed him for the task; he was still a young boy. He had to grow into his crown by serving as a shepherd, a warrior, a musician, and even as a refugee. (Check out 1 Samuel 16:12 and 1 Samuel 19–24.) As Saul was chasing David down, attempting to kill him, David must have wondered if God had really spoken through Samuel when he said David would be the next king. The process did not make any sense and was more than just a little confusing and worrisome.

Sometimes God delays us and allows the fog to come in for positive reasons—so we can minister to those who would have gone overlooked, so we can meet those whom we would have missed, and so we can grow into the tasks He has planned for us later on.

At other times God allows the fog to set in because we are going the wrong way entirely. Maybe you are applying for the wrong job or are trying to plan the wrong trip, or you are planning on attending the wrong college. Perhaps God is allowing the fog to cloud your life so you don't make a mistake. Sometimes He prevents us from being where we *want* to be so we can end up where we are *supposed* to be.

GOD'S AGENDA

His methods may vary, but His purpose is always the same—He lets us worry and be confused until we realize our situation doesn't make sense because we were being guided by the wrong plan. The lights come on and the fog clears once He explains the new path He has set before us. Sometimes relief comes immediately; other times it comes after a lot of heartache.

Just look at Mary—she was thinking about saving her son from whatever harm may befall Him while He was separated from her, and He was thinking about saving the world. Mary had to learn that God had a *different agenda* than she did. Once she began to understand that, the fog probably cleared for her too—but it may have only been a momentary relief.

Sometimes God briefly rolls the fog back to give us a glimpse of His plan—and then He seemingly takes His hand away and lets the sky cloud over again, leaving us in the dark. But He never leaves us alone.

In high school I wanted to play softball more than anything. I am a huge baseball fan (go Red Sox!), I love to play the game, and I really enjoy being part of a team. What I didn't know at the time was that God had a *different* kind of team in mind for me. If I had made the softball squad freshman year, I wouldn't have been able to commit to going on a missions trip that would take me away for a big portion of the season. I couldn't start at second base if I was traipsing through Europe sharing the Gospel.

But that wasn't clear to me at the time, and the fog

rolled in. On the first morning of tryouts I woke up with a 101-degree fever. By the second day I was a little better, but I still wasn't well enough to play my best and make the team. I was devastated at first—until I got to Europe and saw what God had for me there as I participated in street dramas and vacation Bible school, led Hungarians to Christ, and made some lifelong friends.

I only saw God's purpose *after* the fact. The day I got cut from the team I cried my eyes out in the locker room, unable to understand why God wouldn't let me play a game I loved.

It was the same way a few years later when I lost a narrow race for senior-class president only to be named editor-in-chief of the yearbook staff a few weeks later. God knew my strength was in writing and not politics, so He let the fog set in as I sat in bewilderment, wondering what went wrong in my campaign. According to God, nothing went wrong. Everything went right, and I was finally on the right track.

But no matter what God's reason is or what method He chooses to use, His *purpose* in allowing us to be temporarily blinded by the fog is always the same: to build faith in those He loves and to strengthen the character of those He has called.

Early on Mary had to be introduced to the fact that raising Jesus would be different than raising His brothers so she wouldn't be caught off guard one day when Jesus left home and began His earthly ministry. She had to endure repeated periods of fog in order to understand that Jesus' role in the salvation of this world was even more complicated, and far bigger, than she imagined. God knew Mary would need to have her faith built early on so she would be ready to deal with the Cross when it came. Perhaps God is building faith in you, as He leads you through the fog in your life, for something He knows lies ahead.

Paul, Joseph, Ruth, and David all had to endure delays and route changes unique to them in order to step into the roles God had predetermined for them. Have you been slowed down or redirected lately? Then take heart, because you are being prepared for something that will cause all this confusion to make sense sometime in the future.

WHEN GOD FINALLY APPEARS

What is fog, anyway? It is simply low clouds. That's encouraging to me because God has been known to show up in clouds! Genesis 9:13 tells us it's where He set His rainbow as a sign of His covenant to Noah. Exodus 34:5 says it's where He appeared to Moses and spoke to him face to face as a friend. Nahum 1:3 even tells us the clouds are the dust of God's feet.

I opened this chapter with a foggy beach scene in which my mom was reminded of just how quickly the fog can come in and blanket us with confusion. In John 21:1–8 there is another beach scene telling a similar story. After Jesus was crucified and resurrected, the disciples returned to fishing. Although He had made a few appearances to them, they still didn't understand the concept of Jesus establishing a heavenly kingdom rather than an earthly one.

WORRY AND CONFUSION ARE GOD'S TOOLS TO DRIVE US INTO HIS LOVING ARMS.

It was early in the morning, just as day was breaking, when they happened to glance toward the shore. Through the foggy mist they saw a figure standing on the beach. At first they did not recognize Him, but for John the fog suddenly lifted and he exclaimed, "It is the Lord." Hearing this, Peter grabbed his outer garment and dove into the water, swimming the whole one hundred yards so he could get to Jesus as quickly as possible.

When God is at work in our lives, we may not be able to recognize Him at first, especially when the fog sets in, worry nags at our hearts, and we are confused. But usually if we look closely, we can see the fingerprints of God on our situation. At that point, what is our response? Do we stay in the boat and slowly make our way to shore like the other disciples? Or do we dive in head first like Peter, rushing to our Lord as fast as we can?

Worry and confusion are God's tools to strengthen our faith. But they are also God's tools to drive us into His loving arms. At times it may seem as if nothing is worse than not knowing what's going on or what's going to happen next. I am sure we all have moments where we wish we could hit Fast Forward to see how everything turns out in the end. But unfortunately (or maybe it's fortunately) we can't do that. We have to take things one step at a time, and sometimes in the fog we can't even see the next step we are taking.

Poor Mary, I think she must have spent her *whole life* in a fog. I often wonder if she ever really knew all that was going on while Jesus was here on earth. Sure, she heard Him say seemingly strange things about being in His Father's house, and His mother and brothers being those who follow Him. But did she ever come to know what that fully meant before the Cross?

When I look at the big picture of her life, I can see God revealing the story to her in pieces—but I am not so sure she knew she was getting the plan in pieces at the time. She probably had moments when she finally felt like she was beginning to "get it" and then ... the fog would return. Like us, Mary must have had many moments when she wanted to grab her head and scream, *God, what are you doing?!*

God does not always expect us to understand. He knows our minds are finite; there are just some things we cannot understand and others that we were not meant to understand. He will never punish us for not understanding, but there will be a consequence if we fail to trust and obey Him.

In one of my old journals I copied a quote from Amy Carmichael. I'm not sure where it came from exactly, but she said, "He never asked us to understand, just to obey." Mary's life embodies that principle. Sure, there are gaps in her story, and we have only a fraction of information about what really went on in her life, but we always see her being faithful. Despite the fog, the worry, and the confusion, we see her at the cross and we see her ministering among the believers long after Jesus returned to heaven.

To me, that's not a girl who got *lost* in the fog. It's not a girl who was so worried and confused that she gave up and quit. And Mary definitely was not one who sat here on earth and demanded answers from God. No, Mary was more like Peter on the beach that morning in John 21. She took advantage of every moment she had with her Lord. She loved Him—and when she was worried and confused we see her frantically searching for Jesus. As long as she had Jesus, everything was okay.

AS LONG AS SHE HAD JESUS, EVERYTHING WAS OKAY.

The same is true for us. In the midst of the fog we may feel as if we too have lost sight of Jesus. We may not recognize His hand at work in our lives. We may feel cold, alone, and bewildered. And in certain moments we may even find ourselves too tired to take the next step.

But He is always there just the same, whether we see Him or not. I remember the first time I panicked because I could not "feel" God. I was at a youth camp and everyone else was crying and having emotional responses to the teaching and worship. I wanted to feel something so badly. I was gleaning so much knowledge from the messages being taught, yet I couldn't even force tears when I tried. I felt like I was in a fog and was being prevented from seeing God in a way everyone else was.

But God steadily and quietly ministered to my heart, saying, "Shannon, I am not an emotion." There was nothing wrong with everyone else's tears, but there was also nothing wrong with my lack of tears. Even when I could not "feel" God, He was there just the same.

Take a look at the foggy beach of your life right now. Are you worried about the future and confused about what's going on? Take heart, and look for the One who meets us in the fog. He's there when we can't see Him; He's there when we can't hear Him; and He's even there when we can't feel Him. Even though He doesn't answer all of our questions, He will always reveal who He is— and that is more than enough for us.

9

WHEN EXPECTATIONS
DON'T DELIVER

*"When the wine ran out, the mother
of Jesus said to Him, 'They have no wine.'"*
—John 2:3

I vividly remember the lonely nights I spent crying myself to sleep during my first year of college. I was away from home, had recently had my heart broken, and school was harder than I thought it would be. My expectations for a fun-filled, carefree college experience were slowly slipping away and disappointment was setting in.

I loved God and really wanted to live a life pleasing to Him. I had chosen to go to a Christian college because of that, but nothing seemed to be going right for me. That's when I began to learn that, many times, expectations do nothing but set us up for a fall.

I'm sure Mary had her share of unfulfilled expectations too—not because God was not faithful, but because she was looking for God to do something different. Have you experienced any unfulfilled expectations lately? Perhaps you have found yourself sadly uttering, "God could have ... but He didn't."

My friend Laura was recently a contestant on the TV show *Wheel of Fortune.* Before she went on the show she made a commitment to our friend Matt to donate 10 percent of whatever she won to his translation project. He is in the process of translating theology books into Spanish so pastors outside the United States can have access to the same wealth of information we have here. Matt was stoked.

During the beginning of the show Laura was on a hot streak. The numbers in her "bank account" kept getting higher and higher as she spun the wheel and guessed the right letters. But then she hit a snag and time after time she landed on the infamous "Lose a Turn" and "Bankrupt" spaces. She left the show that day in last place— with only $3,000 in cash. Matt's e-mail to Laura and me, sent on the night the show aired, reflected all of our feelings.

"[In some ways] I really struggle with what happened ... so many close calls. God knew what the money was to be used for; He could have moved the wheel to ten thousand dollars, but He did not. I will never understand that," he wrote, "just as I never understood when I did not win the lottery when it was for ten million dollars."

Although there is some humor in what Matt said, there is also an underlying truth that stings. What are we supposed to do when the bottom falls out and we know God could have prevented it? How are we supposed to have faith in a God who does not always do all that He could for us?

I WASN'T EXPECTING THIS!

Back in Mary's day the Jewish people had a very specific expectation for the Messiah to come. They were looking for a man of political influence and earthly valor—in other words, a warrior king. The concept of a dying Savior who would later be resurrected was foreign to them. And to Mary too. *The International Standard Bible Encyclopedia*[1] says:

> The whole Jewish literature agrees on only one feature of the Messiah: he will be a political ruler and national hero. His saving power requires that he deliver Israel from its oppressors and restore the authority of the law.

It goes on to say that Jews at that time took the Old Testament features placed on Yahweh, the warrior and conqueror, and placed them on the Messiah. For sure, they wouldn't have been expecting someone like Jesus.

On the day Mary found herself "blessed among women," she was not expecting someone destined to be crucified to come through her womb. Like everyone else, she was expecting a kingly Messiah who would set the record straight and free the Jews from the leadership of Rome.

Imagine Mary's disappointment, her despair, on the day she saw Jesus hanging on the cross. There was nothing that said "warrior" at Christ's crucifixion. Every bit of hope she had probably died with Him that day. Not only was she not liberated from Rome, she was now also without her son, whom she loved. And for thirty-six painstaking hours she could not see past Golgotha to the resurrection.

On a smaller scale, I am sure we have all had similar moments—moments like Mary had at the wedding at Cana, when she went to Jesus asking for wine and He simply answered her with, "My hour has not yet come." Jesus took care of the lack of wine at the wedding that day, but He did not reveal himself to be the Messiah. (Some scholars say Mary was hinting at this when she asked Him to fix the problem.) Jesus' first miracle was not a huge extravaganza like many would have expected it to be. Instead, only Jesus, the servants, His disciples, and Mary knew what transpired. Here we see that Jesus did not set out to be a national hero like the Jews were looking and hoping for.

There have been many moments in my life when I have asked God for one thing but have received another. Just as Mary looked at the death of her son and saw only defeat, I have looked with despair at the death of my hopes and dreams. I've experienced the pain of un-answered prayers—or at least prayers that were answered in a way I was not expecting.

And I can almost bank on the fact that you have too. (If you haven't yet, you most certainly will.) Perhaps your disappointment came in the form of a broken relation-ship with someone you loved, or maybe it came when someone you were praying for died instead of being healed. Perhaps it came when you did not get into the college of your choice or when your parents divorced or when someone you prayed earnestly for did not come to Christ. Or disappointment may have come in something as simple as not getting asked to the prom.

What are we supposed to do with pain when it comes? And how can we prevent it in the future? Are promises like Psalm 37:4, which says, "Delight yourself in the LORD; and He will give you the desires of your heart," still true when the heartache comes? The answer is a resounding *yes*.

My Wish List

When I first entered college I had a set of expectations I never told anyone about, but I silently set my heart and my mind in that direction. Somewhere I had heard that those of us who choose a Christian college are guaranteed a "ring by spring" or we get our money back. I knew it was a joke, but I also knew a very high percentage of college students fall in love and get married in their college years. I desperately wanted to be one of those students.

I didn't really date in high school, having made a strong commitment to remain pure. So I found it only fitting that God would bring me a godly husband in college to *reward me* for my faithfulness. Once I saw a bumper sticker that said, "Man plans, God laughs." And Psalm 2:4 even says, "He who sits in the heavens laughs." He was most likely laughing at my desire to graduate from college with both a B.A. and an MRS degree.

Not only did I graduate from college without a ring *and* without a boyfriend, but my college years were also virtually dateless. I was busy with work, school, and ministry opportunities—not to mention having fun with friends—which I would have missed out on had I been spending my time dating.

But there were moments during my three and a half years of college when my heart actually hurt because my expectations were not being fulfilled. It wasn't always comforting to think, *Well, the one God has for me is just somewhere else at the moment.*

HE SET MY EXPECTATIONS IN THE RIGHT DIRECTION— TOWARD HIM.

I attended many weddings of not only some of my college friends but also my childhood and high school friends, and I always went home wondering when my turn would come. Surprisingly, though, by the time graduation came I wasn't even sad about the way things turned out for me. I wouldn't have wanted a ring at that moment even if one had been offered to me. Somewhere in the midst of my initial heartache I turned my face back toward Jesus, and He set my expectations in the right direction—toward Him.

Throughout my college years God went to great lengths to remind me that He had a specific plan for me. On one particular day, when I was feeling somewhat discouraged, a letter came in the mail from a friend I had not seen in quite some time. Scrawled at the bottom of the letter, in her precious handwriting, was Psalm 138:8: "The LORD will accomplish what concerns me; Your lovingkindness, O LORD, is everlasting; do not forsake the works of Your hands." Promises like that changed my perspective.

No, I didn't graduate college with a husband, a fiancé, or even a boyfriend—but I graduated with a nationwide ministry I could have never imagined on the day I first set foot on campus. Little did I know then that my expectation for a "happily ever after" was far less than what God wanted to give me.

I believe Mary's expectation was for far less than God wanted to give her too. If she was expecting to birth a national hero—like the Jews expected the Messiah to be—it is logical to assume she was expecting an improvement in her earthly life and status. Eternal life—which was God's plan for her—would have been a foreign concept to her at that time.

What we fail to realize as we are busy planning our lives is it's not that our expectations are too big; it's that our God is way too small. We make God out to be less than all He is because we think we know better as we attempt to govern our lives. If we all got to plan our entire lives and live them out exactly according to our expectations, I guarantee we would be disappointed when all was said and done. There have been many times when I had no clue what I was really asking God for, but He did—and thankfully He said no to my pleading requests.

When He was here, Jesus said no to the requests of the Jewish people as well. The Gospels tell us of countless times they asked Him to establish a kingdom or do things differently. In John 6:14–15 some of the Jews proclaimed Jesus as the Messiah after He fed the five thousand, and they rose up to try to make Him their earthly king. John 7:3–4 tells us that Jesus' own two brothers tried to get Him to rush God's clock and proclaim himself the Messiah at the annual Feast of Tabernacles. And in John 10:24 some of His followers encouraged Him to plainly state that He was the Christ.

They were expecting something from Him, and they tried to make Him be exactly who they wanted Him to be. But Jesus did not come to overthrow the Roman government and establish peace on earth for Mary and her people. Rather, He came to overthrow Satan's worldly kingdom, bringing everlasting life and peace to Mary and all who believe in Him.

Sometimes the answers aren't easy to understand. I, like many of you I am sure, have prayed and waited for years to see friends and family members come to Christ. Some of them never do, and it is always so hard for me to deal with and work through.

When Dreams Die

Phil Vischer, the creator of Veggie Tales, spoke at my college graduation. His message is one I will remember for the rest of my life. Hours and even days later my family and friends were still talking about what he had said. I wrote his key points in my journal so I could always refer back to them.

After opening his speech in the voice of Bob the

Tomato, Mr. Vischer addressed a sea of eager graduates on the topic of what happens when you have a dream, God shows up in it and blesses it, and then it dies. Not a very inspirational and uplifting topic, I know, but his message moved a gymnasium full of thousands to their feet in a standing ovation when he was through—probably because all of us had been there at one time or another.

Mr. Vischer calmly spoke of the fourteen years he spent building Veggie Tales and serving God through storytelling, and then his voice broke with emotion as he spoke about Big Idea Productions going bankrupt. He quoted C. S. Lewis saying, "God whispers to us in our joys, and screams at us in our pain."

> "GOD WHISPERS TO US IN OUR JOYS, AND SCREAMS AT US IN OUR PAIN."

The room was so silent you could hear a pin drop. Hundreds of graduates leaned forward in their seats, listening intently as the tassels swayed back and forth on their cardboard caps.

Then Mr. Vischer hit on the key to the problem with our expectations—idols. "When you are pursuing impact," he said, "you are no longer pursuing God, and you have created an idol." He drew the same conclusion about many of the other things we pursue in our lives.

Impact? How could wanting to impact the world for the Lord Jesus Christ be a bad thing? My mind raced as he continued to speak. Sometimes our expectations are nothing but a hindrance in our walks with God because they prevent us from walking closely with God down the path He has for us.

Mr. Vischer began to unpack the theological problem behind statements like, "God can't steer a parked car." Sometimes we are so busy doing and expecting and working to fulfill our own expectations that we don't even give God room to work. And we steer ourselves right out of His will for our lives!

Even someone in a thriving ministry—like Phil Vischer, whose expectations were seemingly good—sometimes has to deal with a heartbreaking blow in order to stay on God's track.

In John 11 we find Jesus at the grave of Lazarus. Both of his sisters came to Jesus separately, saying, "If You had been here, my brother would not have died" (verse 21). Those who believed Jesus to be the Messiah expected Him to heal the sick—not let them die. Verses 33 and 38 tell us Jesus was "deeply moved" by the women's grief. In fact, Jesus even wept. The Greek word for "deeply moved" is equivalent to our English word *perturbed*.

I was confused the first time I found that out. I always thought it was just the human side of Jesus grieving that made Him cry, but one of my college professors explained it to me differently. He said Jesus was perturbed by the lack of faith still evident among the Jews, and specifically Jesus' followers, at this point in His ministry. Jesus had been healing the sick and feeding the crowds and working wonders before the eyes of the people for quite some time. They claimed they believed, but when tragedy struck, instead of turning to Jesus for comfort, they turned to Him with an "If only..."

Even though He was perturbed, Jesus still cast His eyes heavenward and cried aloud, thanking God for hearing Him. Then He called Lazarus out of his grave. He said He prayed aloud "because of the people," so they would know it was God who worked the miracle and believe in Jesus and be saved.

Here was a group of "believers," completely downtrodden by an unfulfilled expectation, pointing an accusatory finger at the Lord, and what does He do? He blows their minds. He grieves over their unbelief, and then He has compassion. How awesome is that? In an even more radical turn of events, when Mary was grieving the loss of Jesus and the death of her expectations, He arose from the grave and conquered death forever.

God Comes Through

I opened this chapter telling you about a painful time in my freshman year of college, when I cried myself to sleep. But I haven't told you the end of the story yet. On one of those nights, long after my roommate fell asleep, when I was alone with God on my side of the dorm room in the wee hours of the morning, I offered up a quick prayer I will never forget.

"God, it has been a rough first year here and college hasn't been all I expected; I am not even sure I am in the right place," I prayed silently. "So if You want me to come back here next year, please give me something to come back to. I don't care what it is; just let me know it is from

You, and I promise I will come back and tough it out."

The very next day I received a phone call, telling me I was hired for an on-campus job I had applied for; I had to go in for orientation that evening. At orientation I met Heidi, Jessi, and Sam—three of the best friends I have ever had. They became my accountability group as we met every Saturday night at Starbucks for over a year. We took trips together and talked about the hard things in our lives. Being with them provided a place for me to cry, and it gave me a reason to laugh. Even now with miles separating us, I still treasure the friendship we share through phone calls, e-mails, surprise packages, and annual getaways.

TRUSTING GOD IN THE FACE OF DISAPPOINTMENT IS THE ULTIMATE TEST OF FAITH.

The joy of my friendship with them, and the delight that filled my remaining college years, was so much sweeter because I had to travel through the depths of unfulfilled expectations before I could appreciate what God had for me there. Imagine Mary's joy when God revealed His eternal plans for her. There was to be life after death—it doesn't get any sweeter than that!

Disappointment is never God's fault. It is always our fault for assuming too much and knowing too little. God does not promise us all the answers along the way; He simply promises us abundant life (John 10:10) and what is *best* in the end. Those are the things we need to cling to when we are disappointed and we just don't understand. Trusting God in the face of disappointment is the ultimate test of faith. Anybody can walk away when life gets tough. Anyone can be a Sunday morning Christian. But very few know what it takes to survive out on the battlefield.

Perhaps you hear the trumpet sounding as you are being called to battle today. Maybe you are weary, tired, and hurting, and you feel as if you have nothing in you to fight with. Your faith may even be wavering in the face of apparent defeat. Perhaps you feel like Mary on the night they buried Jesus—but take heart, because He is risen. We serve a living God who delights in doing things greater than we can imagine.

We serve a God who knows us better than we even know ourselves. Many of us have moments when we think things are not how they are supposed to be. But Elisabeth Elliot once said, "You can trust the Man who died for you." I wrote those words on a piece of paper and taped them inside the cover of my Bible so I would always remember them, no matter what. Trust me; there have been moments when I needed the reminder.

There will be moments when you need the reminder too. We've already discussed how valuable keeping a journal can be to help us track our spiritual journey. It's also a good way to look back and remind ourselves how faithful God has been and to see how some disappointments in our pasts have turned into hidden blessings somewhere along the way.

We also have to learn to look for the humor in the situations surrounding us. After all, if the Bible says that

God laughs, then I want to be laughing with Him. Ruth Graham, wife of evangelist Billy Graham, put a humorous spin on expectations when she said, "If God answered all of my prayers I would have married the wrong man many times."

NO ROOM FOR IDOLS

Some situations, however, don't leave room for a lot of humor. Sometimes unfulfilled expectations come from sin that has not been dealt with. It can be our own sin or the sin of someone else.

According to the Bible, Abraham was a man of great faith. He waited years for God to make good on His promise that he and his wife, Sarah, would have a son. Years later, after Isaac was born, God gave Abraham some time to really grow to love the boy, and then He asked Abraham to put Isaac on the altar.

> EVERYTHING WE HAVE IS EITHER A TOOL OR AN IDOL.

I've heard it preached that Abraham's love for Isaac was so strong that it was beginning to rival Abraham's love for God. And like Phil Vischer said, anything we are pursuing (or thinking about, or wishing for) more than God has become an idol in our lives. And the Bible makes it clear that idolatry is sin.

Exodus 20:3–4 says, "You shall have no other gods before Me. You shall not make for yourself an idol." Everything we have is either a tool or an idol.

With each painstaking step Abraham took on his

climb toward the altar, he wished for another way—and in the end God provided a ram for the sacrifice, and Isaac lived. But God held Abraham's dream up to his face and asked him if he could trust God as he watched it die.

What happens when there is no ram? Every time I have placed my dreams on the altar and have been honest before God as I watched them burn, God has given me beauty for ashes, like it talks about in Isaiah 61:3. Time after time, He has brought me something *greater* than what I gave.

God didn't ask Abraham to sacrifice Isaac as a means of mocking Abraham's faith or to hurt him. He did it because He loved Abraham with a jealous passion and He wanted Abraham's *whole* heart. God's heart is aflame with passion for you as well. You make God smile, you make His heart race. He loves you with a jealous love—a love that won't let anything come between the two of you. Do you love Him like that?

There is no room for idols in the hearts of those loved by God. You cannot be used greatly by God when you love something—anything—more than you love Him. He will not allow it, at least not for long. Sometimes unfulfilled expectations are a direct result of idols we have built in our lives. When we become consumed with something else, God must obliterate the idol in order to get our attention. He is not doing this to be mean. He is doing it because He loves you.

Perhaps you have recently seen a relationship, a ministry, or some other type of dream destroyed in your life. Let me ask you something I have asked myself many times: Was that dream, that person, or that ministry your idol? It doesn't matter how good it was. It doesn't matter how much glory you thought God could get from it. If you loved it more than God, or even as much as God, it was an idol. But the good news is God forgives as soon as you repent of it. Rest assured, your wounds will heal. God has something *better* for you. And that something better is Him and His plan for your life—whatever it may be.

Our Small Expectations

Maybe your unfulfilled expectation doesn't come from the loss of an idol. Instead, it may be like Mary's— an expectation that was simply too small. Mary expected a Messiah who would bring a little bit of heaven to earth and establish an earthly kingdom. Instead, God provided a way to bring Mary to heaven to live in His kingdom— a kingdom that would last forever. She expected her son to rule for the rest of her lifetime, but His rule is far greater than that. He will rule for all eternity.

"Don't put God in a box," my mom used to tell me. But somehow I always seemed to anyway, and I have often found my dreams and plans were far too small. Like Mary, I have found myself expecting far less from God than He wanted to give.

Not that long ago, when I found myself surprised by the blessings of God that came through unfulfilled expectations, I adopted a new "life verse." Ephesians 3:20 says God is able to do "far more abundantly beyond all that we ask or think, according to the power that works within us."

Take your expectations to God today, and examine them in the light of His glory. Is there something you love today more than you love Jesus? If so, be like Abraham and place it on the altar. Give it over to God fully, and give Him room to work in your life.

When I was growing up, there was a plaque that hung on the bathroom wall at my friend Krissy's house. On it was the famous saying, "If you love something, set it free, and only if it comes back was it ever meant to be." If you let go of something and place it on the altar of your life because you believe that is God's will, be willing to surrender it completely. Expect to never see that dream or wish—or whatever—again. But if it is part of God's will for your life, you will get it back—most likely tenfold.

And if you examine your life and find you do love Jesus more than your expectations but you are still disappointed, remember Mary and her small expectations. God wants to do for you more than you could ever imagine. He wants to give you more than your hands could ever hold. He wants to give you exceedingly abundantly above all you could ask or think. And He wants to give you life abundantly. Notice, God repeatedly uses the word *abundant* when it comes to what He wants to give us.

All you have to do is look to Him and let Him do it His way. The Savior that Mary was expecting was far too small. What kind of Savior are you expecting today?

10

THOUGHT OF ON THE CROSS

"When Jesus then saw His mother, and the disciple whom He loved standing nearby, He said to His mother, 'Woman, behold, your son!' Then He said to the disciple, 'Behold, your mother!' And from that hour the disciple took her into his own household."
—John 19:26–27

I was fifteen and terrified. For months I had been sick and in excruciating pain, and test results only produced more questions. My tears—which I could no longer keep hidden—drove those who loved me to their knees in prayer. On one cold, dark afternoon, as the distant sun sank behind the trees, I sat looking out the window and pondered the recent phone call from my doctor.

God, where are You? My mind desperately searched for a sign of God's love I could cling to. I smoothed my hands over my silk pajama pants and winced in pain as I shifted my legs. My hand instinctively flew to the protruding bump on my abdomen and I fought back tears as

I thought of the surgery my doctor had just scheduled for the next week.

I'm tougher than this, I thought. *I can't cry now.* But I melted into a sobbing puddle before the night was over. There was nothing anyone could do to console me—until God met me in the pages of Genesis.

Thousands of years earlier, on another dark afternoon, after forty days of a wicked downpour of water and wrath, God set a rainbow in the clouds to remind His friend Noah that He would not flood the earth again and that He was continually with him.

A few days after my tearful explosion, I cast a look at the literally stormy skies above me and quietly asked, *Lord, where's my rainbow?* Biting my bottom lip, I entered the hospital for an operation that would decide my fate.

Hours later, after a more extensive surgery than had been originally planned, some of the top surgeons in the state emerged from the operating room to inform my parents that my recovery would be long and grueling—but I would be fine.

Later, as I was being wheeled from recovery to my own hospital room, I remember telling my mom I thought I was going to die—my body was wracked with pain and my mind was fuzzy from medication. Before I even realized what was happening, my dad flew into my hospital room and threw back the curtains to reveal the brightest and most brilliant rainbow the San Diego sky has ever seen.

People all over the hospital were talking about it, but I knew it was for me. That rainbow was God's gift to a fifteen-year-old girl who was unsure of whether or not she could survive what was next. It was my personal reminder God was with me and He was thinking of me. Imagine that: God was thinking of *me*!

Long before God ever lit my sky with a rainbow, another girl was on His mind in the midst of *His* most excruciating hour. As Jesus hung on the cross dying, He looked into the crowd of spectators and He saw the tear-stained face of Mary.

Suddenly, His thoughts were not on His burdens. They weren't even focused on the world. For one brief moment all Jesus could think of was a girl—a girl He loved. And in the raspy whisper of a nearly dead man, He uttered one final statement of His love.

"Woman, behold your son. . . ." And looking at John, His beloved disciple, He said, "Behold your mother." That was Jesus' way of making sure Mary would be well taken care of for the rest of her life. It was His way of *showing* His love for her. In that statement Jesus reached out with His heart when He couldn't physically reach out with His nail-pierced hands.

Oh, how joy must have mingled with Mary's pain in that moment. Her heart must have warmed as the gaze of her beloved Jesus met hers one last time. His face was beaten and marred beyond recognition, but His lingering eye contact must have spoken volumes to the one who knew Him well.

Her heart must have danced as the voice of the One she knew well addressed her one final time. Jesus was dying—but He was thinking of Mary and how He loved her so. Have you ever had a moment that powerful, that poetic, that piercing? Has God ever met you in a moment so outrageously intimate that you knew you would never be the same, no matter what?

Mary wasn't the only one Jesus thought of on the cross that day. Being fully God—and fully man—Jesus was omnipresent. That means He was not constrained by the bounds of time. Although the Bible doesn't say it explicitly, in the six hours He hung on the cross I would venture to guess Jesus' mind hit Fast Forward and He looked ahead to all those He was dying for—to those who would accept His precious sacrifice.

But I don't see Jesus looking ahead to the sins that sent Him to the very cross He was hanging on. The Jesus I know probably looked ahead to the moment each of us would come to know Him and love Him as Lord. To Him, thoughts like that would have made all the pain worth it. The sight of your smiling (and possibly tear-stained) face on the day you first met Jesus was enough to dull the piercing pain of Calvary's cross. It's why He went to the cross in the first place. Hebrews 12:2 says, "Fixing our eyes on Jesus, the author and perfecter of faith, who for the joy set before Him endured the cross, despising the shame, and has sat down at the right hand of the throne of God." Jesus looked to the cross with *joy* because of His love for you.

God loved each one of us enough to leave the riches of heaven and reside in the utter poverty of this earth. He didn't even come to an earthly palace. Nor did He come as someone who merited the world's respect. Imagine:

God came to earth as a *nobody* in hopes of making you *somebody*. But on most days it doesn't even seem as if you care.

Zephaniah 3:17 says that God rejoices and sings over you. That's better than any love song you could ever hear on the radio. Isaiah 49:16 talks about God inscribing us on the palms of His hands. He does not forget about us and He does not give up on us. Romans 5:8 tells us that it was while we were still sinners that Christ died

> GOD CAME TO EARTH AS A NOBODY IN HOPES OF MAKING YOU SOMEBODY.

for us; we did not even have to clean up our act before coming to God. We have never once had to earn God's love, and we never will.

YOU WERE ENOUGH FOR HIM

Yes, Jesus died for the sins of this world. But He would have died just for you. He would have given everything in an attempt to win *your* heart—and as much as we may try to avoid the facts, He did give everything.

To God, you were enough. You were the one thing missing from paradise. You were the one thing keeping heaven from being perfect. In God's opinion, heaven wasn't home without you. Is God enough for you? Do you live like you truly believe He is?

Yes, God called a girl. But more important, He *loved* a girl. He loved Mary—and when Jesus was hanging on the cross He sure let her know it. Jesus devoted several of

His last breaths to assuring Mary that she would be loved and cared for. He loves you just as much, and He goes to great lengths to let you know it too. Do you realize it—or do you walk around with blinders on?

IN GOD'S OPINION, HEAVEN WASN'T HOME WITHOUT YOU.

During my junior year of college, I was sharing a *one*-bedroom apartment with *two* other girls. One was engaged, the other was soon to be engaged, and I wasn't even dating anyone. On Valentine's Day our apartment was flooded with flowers, balloons, chocolate, and stuffed animals—none of which were for me. You couldn't walk two feet without tripping over a pesky reminder that love was in the air. My friend Amy stopped by one afternoon and surveyed my pathetic state without saying a word.

It wasn't until a few nights later, at Bible study, that I even realized she had noticed a small florist had overtaken my living room. She walked in that night with a dozen roses of various colors.

"This idea was inspired by Shannon," she said, handing each of us a rose. Mine was pink—my favorite color. "God sends you flowers each morning as a symbol of His love for you," she said. "It's up to you whether you receive them or not."

Something about that moment resonated deep within me, and I will never forget how moved I was by what she said. Sure, I didn't have some hot guy knocking himself out to get my attention—but I did have the God of the universe madly and totally in love with me. How had I overlooked that fact?

We have no reason to feel unloved—ever. Not when we get dumped, not when we are betrayed by our best friend, not when our parents belittle our dreams or when our teachers put down our most valiant efforts.

Each morning God calls out to us—but most of the time we are too busy to notice or too self absorbed to care. We take Christ's sacrifice on Calvary's cross lightly. We are consumed with thoughts of everything we want, and we fail to realize we already have *more* than we could ever need.

Through the Eyes of Love

When we place other things above the Lord in our lives, we are sending a loud and clear message that what Christ did on the cross was not enough for us. We walk around and give our hearts to those who give us much less. What is wrong with us? We have been written into the greatest love story

> WE WANT A CARTOON WHEN WE HAVE THE REAL THING.

of all time, yet we are still looking out the window, wishing we were Cinderella. Think of that: We want a cartoon, a mere figment of someone else's imagination, when we have the real thing. How terribly sad.

Is this how we are going to live the rest of our lives—dreaming of fairytale castles when we have been invited to the one true palace? Deep inside I think most of us feel like nothing more than fraudulent princesses. *God can't be in love with me*, we think as we try in vain to cover the dark and ugly parts of ourselves from the world's view. Deep inside we dream huge dreams of being—or belonging to—somebody, yet on the outside we paint plastic smiles on tear-stained faces.

We live in a world that has trained us to see nothing but our flaws. The first thing we see in the mirror is volcano-sized pimples, crooked noses, and Dumbo ears. But when God looks at us He sees perfection—not because He sees us as we are, but because He sees us for who we can be in light of His love for us. His love makes us elegant. His love makes us beautiful. His love gives us purpose and reveals to us who we truly are.

Perhaps you have traveled the pages of Mary's story with me, feeling as if God could never call you, or love you, like that. As I write this chapter, I am experiencing the beauty of a rainbow-colored sunset from an airplane window. I am flying from the East Coast to the West Coast, and we have been chasing the sun for hours.

Brilliant oranges, pinks, and purples are topping off the majestic blue that normally blankets the earth. It's a real work of art. I wish I could take a picture and capture its beauty forever. My breath is literally taken away as I look at it.

That's what happens when God thinks of you—you captivate Him. You light God's world with a rainbow-colored sunset. You are a work of art, even though some people may tell you that you are a real piece of work!

Like the clay the potter used to make great and beautiful things in Jeremiah 18:3–4, God desires to use you to do great and beautiful things in the world around you. Just as God delighted in Mary, so He delights in you. Remember, He wants to use you in the process of blessing you. The opportunities before you are endless. You just need to let God work as He pleases in your life, like Mary did. You must learn to let Him have His way when your paths are lined with bright blooming flowers *and* when you are led through parched and barren deserts.

But before you can be a girl called by God to impact the world, you must come to accept the joy of being a girl God loves. The joy of the Lord shall be your strength, as it says in Nehemiah 8:10. You must learn to let God love you. As fallible human beings, we are not accustomed to letting anyone love us unconditionally. We are used to affection that comes with strings attached. Love usually comes to us only when we earn it.

A NEW START

During my sophomore year of college I was hit with an epiphany one night as I sat alone in the dim light of my dorm room in Alpha Chi. No one else was around. For a brief moment there was nobody to please, nobody's love to earn.

For the first time in months I let the tears flow freely. I had been trying so hard to get someone to love me that I had forgotten Someone *did* love me. At nineteen years old, my focus was on being popular and well liked and trying to convince someone—anyone—to fall in love with me.

That night, in brokenness, I decided to start over. I made a commitment to accept the love God was waiting to lavish upon me—and to let that be enough. That night I *chose* to stop performing, stop competing, and to fully surrender to the Lord. I acknowledged that although I didn't have everything I wanted, I had everything I needed—and for that I was eternally grateful. As a way of making my new commitment to God "official," I poured my heart out to Him in a poem. I titled it "New Start." It goes like this:

> *I come to the altar with no Isaac to bring*
> *Just the desire to be loved and the hope for a ring*
> *I've waited, I've worried, and I have failed to trust*
> *So take from me this desire and teach me as You must*
> *All alone before You, my heart I spill*
> *With laughter and tears this empty vessel fill*
> *I am looking, Lord, no longer for a man*
> *But now to You, and what You have planned*
> *I am gifted and growing and I want to serve You*
> *Just show me where to go and who to serve as I seek*
>   *to follow through*
> *And if alone You want me, for years to come*
> *Isolate and teach me what is to be done*
> *I can't fight You any longer, I am too weak*
> *I am done with fool's gold and real treasure I seek*
> *I want You, O Lord, to put a twinkle in my eye*
> *I want You to be my focus and not any other guy*
> *But even as I say this, part of me holds back*
> *Help me to see that singleness is a blessing and not an attack*
> *Lord, help me not to feel worthless, unblessed, and alone*
> *Help me to throw my cares at the foot of Your throne*

As You want me to wait, Lord, please put a hold on my heart
Help me not to give it away to someone who will tear it apart
As I lay my desire down at Your feet
Help me to be honest and my promises keep
Help me in loneliness to focus on the Cross
And when I feel left out, help me count it as loss
I don't want to struggle; I am too tired to fight
Help me to keep on and do what is right
Remove from me this jealousy and replace it with joy
Fill my thoughts with You, O Lord, instead of a boy
On the altar of sacrifice I place my desire
And I ask, Lord, right now that You'd burn it with fire
Please accept it, O Lord, for it is all I have to give
Help me to let go of this bondage and truly live
Take all of me, Lord, even when I am opposed
Help me to trust in You, the One who always knows
On my knees I fall, with tears on my face
And I ask, Lord, only that You'd meet me in this place
Altars are for bloodshed so, Lord, here's my heart
Take it from me now, and grant me a new start.

Each of us has moments when we are desperately in need of a new start.

Mary was on the brink of a new start as she stood at the foot of the cross. Her whole world was changing and there was nothing she could do to stop it. Perhaps you feel the same way.

As He hung on the cross dying, Jesus had one final phrase to utter to Mary. Right now, He has a phrase He is uttering to you as well. *Precious daughter,* He says, with a smile playing at the corners of His mouth, *I will never leave you or forsake you. Delight yourself in Me and I will give you the desires of your heart.* I suggest you highlight and memorize verses like Deuteronomy 31:6 and Psalm 37:4 as a way of holding on to that message.

God has mapped out an exciting journey for you. You will impact the world in a way that will be revealed to you piece by piece, just like Mary's was. You too will leave your mark on history; I don't doubt that even for a moment. But in order to overcome your questions and fears, before you can be obedient and amazed, and even in spite of being disappointed and shut out—you must let God pull back the heavens and rain His love down on you.

> ONE FAITHFUL GIRL IS ALL GOD NEEDS TO START A REVOLUTION.

Let the reality that God loves you, more than anyone else ever could, change you at the very core of your being. Allow it to affect the way you see yourself every time you look in the mirror. *You* are the beloved of God.

Jesus thought of *you* on the cross. And you have been thought of every day since. The Creator of the universe is also the Creator of your very soul. He created you for a purpose. *You* are destined for greatness.

The thought of *you* was enough to keep the King of Kings strung up on a Roman cross; think of that the next time you wonder about what one girl can do. It only takes one to shake a nation. It only takes one to change the world. One faithful girl is all God needs to start a revolution.

In time one can easily become one hundred, one thousand, or one million. But you can't have one hundred, one thousand, or one million without first having one.

You are that one. So what are you going to do about it?

Acknowledgments

Life is a team sport. Victory is never achieved alone. From those who take the field with you to those who sit in the stands and cheer, the people in your life play an incredible role in whether you win or lose.

Much like life, writing a book is a team sport. And I would like to thank my team. There are too many to mention all of them by name—but they know who they are. A few, though, need to be mentioned by name because their contribution to this book was so great. So here goes . . .

First of all I would like to thank my friend and agent, Janet Kobobel Grant, for partnering with me on this book. Thanks for seeing potential in me and for taking me to a new place in my writing career. I hope this book is the first of many we do together.

I would also like to thank my dear friend Robin Gunn for introducing me to Janet and for encouraging me when I was ready to give up. I am so glad we bumped into each other at Islands that day!

Working with Bethany House Publishers has been an incredible experience for me, and I would like to thank Kyle Duncan for being willing to add just one more project to the Spring 2005 calendar. I would also like to thank Natasha Sperling and Jeanne Hedrick for the insights that sharpened the first draft of this book and made it into the beautiful version you now hold in your hands. And my heartfelt thanks goes to Jennifer Parker for creating such a beautiful cover.

Before this manuscript was ever a book it was a dream—a dream buried deep in my heart. A special thanks goes out to my mom and dad, who love me and never doubted this book would find its way into print. And they get extra points because they have to live with me when I am writing on deadline! I love you guys and appreciate all you do for me.

I would also like to thank my Darlin and Papa for reading the manuscript a thousand times over and for praying me through the process. You guys are the best and I love you.

And, of course, I want to thank my sweet Michael. You expand my mind and my heart in ways I never knew anyone ever could. Thanks for reminding me of my calling and for never letting me give up no matter how loudly I whine. You are my best friend and I love you.

I would also like to thank Pastors Brian, Dan, Armando, and Eric for giving me the chance to minister to the awesome girls of Impact Junior High ministry and Wallace High School ministry—the girls are the reason I write books like this in the first place. And thanks to Pastor Todd for loaning me his library.

A special thanks goes out to Dr. Matt Williams at Biola University for teaching the Word of God in such a powerful way and for offering many insights into this book. Thanks for teaching with enthusiasm and for drawing me closer to Jesus.

I would also like to thank Dean and Kathy Blackwelder for the countless times they took me to dinner and listened to me talk passionately about the topics contained in these pages. Thanks for never appearing bored. Next time, dinner is on me.

And to Andrea Stephens, thanks again for another sparkling endorsement.

Most importantly, I would like to thank my Lord and Savior Jesus Christ for gifting and calling me to write. May You find this book to be an offering pleasing in Your sight. I love You most of all!

And last, but certainly not least, I would like to thank you—the reader—for picking up this book and deeming it worth your time. My prayer is that by reading it you come to understand both God's love and God's call just a little more clearly. I would love to hear your thoughts on the book anytime.

Endnotes

Chapter 1

1. R. Kent Hughes, *Luke: Volume One* (Wheaton, IL: Crossway Books, 1998), 30.
2. Barbara Robinson, *The Best Christmas Pageant Ever* (Wheaton, IL: Tyndale Publishers, 1982).

Chapter 2

1. John Eldredge, *The Journey of Desire* (Nashville, TN: Thomas Nelson Publishers, 2000), 180.
2. Eddie Carswell and Bobbie Mason, "Trust His Heart." Word Music Group, Inc., 1989.
3. David Jeremiah, *Sanctuary* (Nashville, TN: Integrity, 2202), 297.
4. Dag Hammarskjöld, *Markings* (New York: Knopf, 1964).

Chapter 3

1. Amy Carmichael, *If* (London: Dohnavur Fellowship, 1938), 57.
2. Hughes, 30.

Chapter 4

1. Craig Dunham and Doug Serven, *TwentySomeone* (Colorado Springs, CO: Waterbrook Press, 2003), 138.

Chapter 5

1. *Disciple's Study Bible.* CD-ROM. QuickVerse Deluxe, Version 7. Parsons Church Group, 2000–2001.
2. *Vincent's Word Studies.* CD-ROM. QuickVerse Deluxe, Version 7. Parsons Church Group, 2000–2001.
3. *Disciple's Study Bible.*
4. Elisabeth Elliot, *Passion and Purity* (Grand Rapids, MI: Fleming H. Revell, 31st ed. 1996), 97.
5. *The Ryrie Study Bible. Believer's Study Bible. Bible Knowledge Commentary. IVP Bible Background Commentary.* CD-ROM. QuickVerse Deluxe, Version 7. Parsons Church Group, 2000–2001.
6. *IVP Bible Background Commentary.* CD-ROM. QuickVerse Deluxe, Version 7. Parsons Church Group, 2000–2001.
7. L. B. Cowman, *Streams in the Desert.* (Grand Rapids, MI: Zondervan, 1997), 174.

Chapter 6

1. Elisabeth Elliot, *The Journals of Jim Elliot* (Grand Rapids, MI: Fleming H. Revell, 1978), 475.
2. Lisa Beamer, *Let's Roll* (Wheaton, IL: Tyndale House, 2002), 274.
3. R. Kent Hughes, *Luke: Volume One* (Wheaton, IL: Crossway Books, 1998), 14–15.

Chapter 7

1. L. B. Cowman, *Streams in the Desert Calendar* (Grand Rapids, MI: Zondervan, 1996).
2. Rich Mullins, *The World As I Remember It: Through the Eyes of a Ragamuffin* (Sisters, OR: Multnomah, 2004), 57.

Chapter 8

1. Sam Wellman, *Gladys Aylward: Missionary to China* (Uhrichsville, OH: Barbour Publishing, Inc.).

Chapter 9

1. Geoffrey Bromiley, *The International Standard Bible Encyclopedia, Volume 3* (Grand Rapids, MI: Eerdmans Publishing Company, 1988), 333.